Fifty Years of Catholic Theology

Fifty Years of
Catholic Theology

Conversations with Yves Congar

Edited and introduced by
Bernard Lauret

SCM PRESS LTD

Translated by John Bowden from the French
Entretiens d'automne,
published 1987 by Les Éditions du Cerf,
29, bd Latour-Mabourg, Paris.

British Library Cataloguing in Publication Data

Congar, Yves
Fifty years of Catholic theology:
conversations with Yves Congar.
1. Catholic theology
I. Title   II. Lauret, Bernard
III. Entretiens d'automne. *English*
230'.2

ISBN 0–334–00472–1

First British edition published 1988
by SCM Press Ltd,
26-30 Tottenham Road, London N1 4BZ

Phototypesetting by Input Typesetting Ltd, London
and printed in Great Britain by
Richard Clay Ltd, Bungay, Suffolk

Contents

	Introduction	1
1	Vatican II. Departure from Tridentinism	3
2	Do We Know Christianity?	22
	Europe and secularization	23
3	The Religions	34
	Islam	34
	Judaism	36
4	The Church	40
5	Faith, Spirituality and Theology	59
	By Way of a Conclusion	86

Introduction

Yves-Marie Congar's first book, *Chrétiens désunis: Principes d'un oecuménisme catholique* (Disunited Christians: Principles for a Catholic Ecumenism), was published in June 1937. It was the firstfruit of an ecumenical spring – still tentative, but now apparently irreversible. These 'principles for a Catholic ecumenism' have stood the test of time. But trees are judged by their fruit. Twenty-five years later saw the opening of the Second Vatican Council, which the extraordinary Synod held in 1985 recognized as having a depth and a prophetic significance which will last for many years to come. The 1985 Synod is the first synod of such magnitude in the history of the church to have been summoned specifically in order to endorse with due solemnity the work of a previous council. Few people during the last half-century have had so intensive a life as Fr Congar – within the church and for the church.

Fifty years after *Chrétiens désunis*, the conversations printed in this book bear witness to the serenity and authority of a man who knows that he has fulfilled his theological task. On 9 October 1984 Fr Congar had to leave Saint Jacques, the Dominican house in which he had been living, and the precious library of Le Saulchoir, for permanent hospital care in the Institution des Invalides in Paris. His work has not stopped: lectures, reviews, articles, various conversations go on, but in a new rhythm punctuated by the demands of hospital routine and numerous visits from his Dominican brothers and from colleagues, students and friends. However, it is no longer possible for him to consult

1

notes, check references or to continue to enrich already well-filled pages with footnotes containing new titles.

So these conversations are unpretentious. They do not set out to assess Fr Congar's work, nor do they get lost in complicated technical questions. At a time when a host of other figures are not slow to make known their opinion on topics debated within the church, his comments are aimed only at raising a voice which has always been concerned for the truth, supported by historical knowledge and firm in the faith. So these conversations are not like a journalistic interview, which has its own rules. Before they began I simply gave Fr Congar a number of questions, most of which appear in the various chapters of the book. I had formulated the questions after consultation with the publishers. This broad canvas served as a background to these conversations, which took place over a period of two years, during brief sessions towards the end of the afternoon at irregular intervals, taking advantage of some of Fr Congar's rare free time. I hope that they will convey, as a testimony of faith, something of that classical spirit embodied in the square, the façade, the courtyards and the buildings of the Invalides in which they took place and which Charles Péguy regarded as 'the finest monument in Paris'.

Bernard Lauret

— 1 —

Vatican II.
Departure from Tridentinism

You are a theologian who played an active part in preparations for the Second Vatican Council, and you proved one of the most decisive of those who worked on its texts. Do you think that the Council was 'imprudent'? Or do you take the opposite view, that it was an advance in the sense of being an appeal to a more profound tradition? In other words, did not the Council's concern to harmonize the faith with the modern world, by paying attention to the signs of the times, hasten the crisis in the Church and more particularly the crisis over religious practices instead of relieving it? Can we now close what some people have described as the parenthesis opened by Vatican II within a typically Roman Catholic tradition of the kind expressed at the Council of Trent and Vatican I?

I would like to begin by saying something about the responsibility of the Council for what people call the crisis. In my view, the Council does indeed bear some responsibility, but that is inseparable from the grace and benefits which it has brought to the Church and even, one might say, to the world. This benefit has mainly taken the form of a departure from Tridentism. By that I do not mean the Council of Trent itself but Tridentinism as it was defined by Giuseppe Alberigo, in particular in his three lectures at the Collège de France. This Tridentinism is a system developed after the Council of Trent under the influence of three very conservative Popes – Paul IV, Pius V and Sixtus Quintus – who were followed by others. It was a system which took in absolutely everything: theology, ethics, Christian behaviour,

3

religious practices, liturgy, organization, Roman centralization, the perpetual intervention of Roman congregations in the life of the Church, and so on. But the system should not be confused with either the Council of Trent or the First Vatican Council, both of which Vatican II often cites. I have given the figures in another book: I think that it is around twenty times in each case. And here I could add a personal recollection. I was involved in the work on the decree on the priesthood, *Presbyterorum Ordinis*; while the decree goes beyond the Council of Trent, since it makes an essential link between the priesthood on the one hand and the apostolate and the episcopate on the other, from the beginning I felt it absolutely essential that there should be a reference to the Council of Trent, because I told myself that if a council like Trent already spoke of the matter, it could not be treated in the abstract. That is a personal example, and I think that it is a significant one. But beyond Trent and Vatican I there is a particular configuration of Roman Catholicism which appeared as a system. The sociologist Jean-Marie Donegani noted it in connection with the decline in Sunday observance:

The first thing that the decline in Sunday observance demonstrates is the massive and irreversible departure of Catholics from the Tridentine universe. The Counter-Reformation was essentially concerned to bring the faithful into line on the basis of an effort at doctrinal clarification and the development of a totalitarian catechesis which divided the world into the thinkable and the unthinkable, the prescribed and the forbidden. This was also, in opposition to the *sola fide*, the beginning of a basis for action of which the birth of Catholic Action is perhaps one of the last phenomena.

This Catholicism disappeared on the death of Pius XII, with the *aggiornamento* of Vatican II and the 'decompression' which followed: 'relaxation of discipline, disappearance of prohibitions, free examination of doctrine, liberation from controls...'

However, I would point that in this quotation the expression 'free examination of doctrine' itself calls for some criticism. I

4

think that what is said is in some ways correct, but the way in which it is put is either too abrupt or too simplistic. It needs to be made more specific. Basically, this idea of the end of Tridentinism fits in very well with what Fr Bouyer in 1968 called the 'decomposition of Catholicism', to quote the title of his book. Another fine book written in 1985 by Yves Lambert, and entitled *God is Changing in Brittany*, describes how this departure from Tridentinism came about in the Brittany parish of Limerzel in the crisis between 1950-1980: the progressive dismantling of a framework which had involved people in a complete system under the authority of the priests. So this process had begun well before the Council, above all as a result of rural Catholic Action. That had brought new developments, but the Council confirmed them.

There has not been enough communication or development of the positive, biblical side of the Council with which a new chapter in the life of the Church really began, albeit one continuous with the living tradition of scripture, the Fathers and the classical centuries. Now the fate of the Church seems to me increasingly to be bound up with a spiritual and even supernatural life, that of the Christian life. I think that in present conditions the only Christians who can stand the pressures are those who have an inner life. Tridentinism represented a kind of conditioning (though I do not mean that in the pejorative sense of the word), I mean a kind of enveloping, the provision of a framework into which one entered and in which one stayed. Whereas today – and this a point to which we shall obviously be returning – given that we live in a secularized world (and one which is particularly influenced by the media), I think that it is impossible to preserve a Christian life-style without a degree of inner life. In this connection I would like to quote a rather strange remark by Fr Émile Mersch, the Belgian Jesuit who made such a contribution to the theology of the mystical body. He said: 'Some animals are surrounded by a shell because they have no skeleton.' I think that today the shell – i.e. the Tridentine system, Tridentinism – has largely dissolved, been sloughed off

5

in some way, and that the need for some kind of inner framework has become all the more imperative.

All the same, in connection with the Council I would like to add a remark which seems to me to be very important and to which we shall be returning when we talk about theology. The Council discussed and worked in commissions – I myself worked in four or five of them, sometimes in several at once – and this work ended up with texts. You will know that there are sixteen documents: two dogmatic constitutions, a pastoral constitution, the constitution on the liturgy and then decrees and declarations. These are texts, i.e. collections of ideas. But the ideas still have to be applied in a specific way. Obviously these ideas themselves have a dynamic of their own. And I believe that the Council really does have a dynamism in this sphere. The fact that some of the ideas may perhaps have been abused does not mean that there was not a real vitality in the Council. But it would be dangerous to think that the composition of texts was all that there was to it. At this point in a way I am making a criticism of myself, since this is a tendency that I can note in my own life: I have often worked as if once one has put forward ideas, that's that. But that is not true: the ideas then have to be put into practice. And to be specific, if the Council has had any significance, it has been that of a transition from the ideal or ideological sphere to the everyday life of the Church. John XXIII was right to say that the Council was 'pastoral'. It has been noted that what John XXIII called 'pastoral' was doctrinal in character, but doctrine expressing itself in history, in time and in the present-day world. Of course there are those who have misused the term by saying, 'Since it is pastoral, it is not doctrinal'. That is quite wrong: the term includes the doctrinal element, but this is doctrinal-pastoral, i.e. doctrinal in terms of a doctrine which requires to be applied historically, which is not a kind of no man's land between heaven and earth, a kind of absolute, unchangeable, untouchable framework. The term does not relate to this last; it has to be applied in a specific way. The personality of John XXIII himself was very significant in this sense. It is an amazing fact that although the pontificate of Pius

6

XII was a most distinguished one, and on many matters he was a truly dominant influence – and he had a very great reputation throughout the world, including the Protestant world – within a few weeks John XXIII had made people 'forget' him. Of course, he was not really ignored. I have already said that the Council often referred to earlier insights – there are 120 quotations from or references to Pius XII in the Council texts – and that is deliberate, to mark the continuity.

In spite of this, John XXIII was something quite different. How and why? Precisely because he was specific. He spoke more on the basis of intuitions of the heart than on that of ideas. Certainly there are the *fioretti*, the 'little flowers', of John XXIII, and there is even a story about him in this connection. (I don't know whether it is true; I hope that it isn't, since in the end it isn't a particularly attractive one.) One day, when receiving our President Édouard Herriot, he is said to have asked him, 'Monsieur President, what divides us? Ideas? They amount to so little!' I don't think that John XXIII – or Roncalli, since at that time he was a nuncio – ever said that. But in spite of everything, John XXIII was the kind of a man for whom ideas were not as it were ready-made schemes to be applied as they are, but were truly realities which had to be lived out pastorally. There were good reasons why he wanted a pastoral council. I would like to tell another story about him here: two cardinals repeated to me what John XXIII had said to them, 'They did not understand me!' What did he mean by that? I don't know, and even the cardinals themselves were not very sure. But I would like to think that he meant: 'They have set to work doing theology, when all I wanted was an adaptation, *aggiornamento*, a pastoral adaptation.' But this was necessarily of a doctrinal kind.

However, what John XXIII said at the opening of the Council raised the question whether or not the Council was in continuity with Trent and Vatican I, or at least the question of how Christian faith can be adapted to our time. For he made the famous distinction: 'The

7

deposit itself is one thing and the form under which these truths are presented is another.' What do you think about that?

Beyond doubt, what could shed light on this question is an authentic notion of Tradition. Tradition is a living reality, and not the material transmission of something to be taken up again as it is. Tradition is a living principle throughout the history of the Church, for everything is historical; I shall have occasion to return to this point later. In passing, let me say that I believe that the novelty of Vatican II consisted largely in its acceptance of the historicity of the Church, of scripture and so on.

To state that these things are historical is certainly not to talk of them as being completely new: one takes up what went before but in unprecedented conditions. That's where the famous adaptation comes in. In the second edition of my short book about Mgr Lefebvre and the crisis of the Church I quoted the splendid letter from Paul VI to Mgr Lefebvre about Tradition. Whereas for Mgr Lefebvre Tradition is Trent and the *Syllabus*, and everything stops there, the Pope explains to him that Tradition is a living reality and not just the material reaffirmation of the past as it was. I am convinced that Vatican II is in the Tradition. But obviously it has brought something new.

Take collegiality, which we shall certainly be discussing in due course. That was already announced in Vatican I. Fr Torrell's thesis on the theology of the episcopate at the First Vatican Council is quite convincing on that point. That has been recognized by Aubert and all the historians of Vatican I. In spite of everything, the point was not developed in any way, since Vatican I made a dogmatic pronouncement only on the papacy and not at all on the episcopate; it had planned to do so, but there was no time. And at the opening of the second session of the Council, Paul VI made a point of saying that Vatican II had completed Vatican I with a theology of the episcopate and of collegiality. So it is not new and yet it is new. Both things are true at the same time.

On the eve of the opening of the extraordinary Synod to celebrate the

8

anniversary of the conclusion of Vatican II, there were those who stressed the continuity of Vatican II with former councils, Trent and Vatican I. Others noted the breaks with former tradition, for example the prohibition of the Mass in the vernacular by Alexander VII or, more important, relations with Judaism, or the status of the people of God, and so on. These are the new developments which appeared with Vatican II.

Certainly. One might also refer to the *Syllabus*, in 1864. This was an extremely distinctive period, marked not only by the general climate – the Church felt itself to be under siege – but also by the personality of Pius IX and his entourage. It is all too clear that it is dated. In christology one might also take, for example, the Council of Chalcedon, which is the great point of reference: you know the fine text, 'without confusion and without separation', where precisions are avoided and a positive statement is made in a negative form. But that was not enough; the sequel was the monotheletism which necessitated the Council of Constantinople in 681 and, even before that, the Lateran Council in 679 – attended by the famous Maximus the Confessor. These councils had to clarify christological issues which had not been brought out at Chalcedon. I think that there is something of an analogy here: we have transmission of the past and still the same principle, but in a new historical situation and clearly with a new spirituality: people have gone on thinking since Trent and Vatican I, and the world has changed. Take the episcopate: at Vatican I there was not a single black bishop, and at Vatican II there were perhaps five hundred of them; today there are seven or eight black cardinals. Things have changed completely.

So rather than settle the question of the relationship between Vatican II and the earlier councils one way or another you would prefer to speak of the historicity of the Church...

Yes, that's not relativism, but it's not opposition to change either.

However, you referred to the question of the episcopate. There are those who say that among the crises opened up by Vatican II, one was the question of the sacerdotal character of the priesthood. One could say that Vatican I left the question of the local church and the collegiality of the episcopate open by not dealing with it, since everything was seen in terms of the Roman pontiff and the universal Church.

In fact this question of the local church and the episcopate was discussed at Vatican II. Similarly, one can say that Vatican II raised the question of the priesthood, though it did not discuss it adequately, since it gave a prominent place to the people of God and the episcopate. Does not Vatican II bear some responsibility here for the crisis among the clergy?

That's a very difficult question to answer. In fact, during the Council itself priests, at any rate in France, kept complaining. They said: 'I'm not a bishop, I'm not a lay person, I'm not a separated brother. No one's interested in me.' That's not true. The bishops were very preoccupied with the question of the priesthood and many of them wrote personally to each of their priests during the Council. That's only a small point, but it's a significant one. And at any rate there was *Presbyterorum Ordinis*. I worked on that text; I drafted some of the paragraphs, above all those at the beginning of the text, but there were too many of us and we had to introduce other ideas. In particular, there was the German contribution.

I know that this isn't enough. On several occasions I've met priests who expressed their dissatisfaction. I told them that there was an idea of priesthood, bound up with the apostolate under the sphere of influence of the bishop. They retorted: Granted, but that's idealistic. That's not what people are asking of us; that's not our experience. And I believe that the crisis is much more of this order: priests are being asked for something other than that for which they were ordained, something other than what they have their hearts in. Particular practical and ceremonial demands are being made on them, the baptism of small children whose parents are not believers, and so on. We

10

all need to be recognized for what we are. In an indifferent world the priest gets hardly any recognition at all and he finds himself in a vacuum.

Is it right to say that episcopal conferences do not have any theological basis, that they have only a 'practical and specific function', and that there is a risk that they will eliminate the personal responsiblity of each bishop? Is such a verdict in accord with the history of the conciliar tradition in the Church and the theology of the local church that one can develop from the texts of Vatican II?

Vatican II certainly led to a reconsideration of the perspective of the local churches in relation to the universal Church. But here we have to distinguish between 'universal' and 'catholic', which people often tend to confuse. Universal is the opposite of particular or local, but catholic is not the opposite of anything. A local church is catholic, and even an individual is catholic; a small community is catholic, but it is obviously not universal. I believe that this rediscovery of the local church which finds remarkable expression in several texts from Vatican II (*Lumen Gentium* no.26, *Christus Dominus* no. 11 and also the text on missions) is extremely important. Karl Rahner even thought it to be the most important part of all the Council's work on ecclesiology. One may differ with him on that, but his verdict stresses how important the matter is.

As for episcopal conferences, I would immediately concede to Ratzinger and also to Fr de Lubac, who discussed this question in a small book a few years ago, that episcopal conferences are not a divine institution like the college or the primacy (the latter, of course, within the college and not above it: *cum et sub Petro*, with and under Peter. *Cum Petro*, let us say, even more than *sub*, but what is called the hierarchical communion is quite acceptable). But while it is true that the episcopal conference is not of divine institution, I would say that the councils are not divine institutions either. Have they only a practical function? I do not think so. It seems to me that they have extremely important theological foundations which are, by analogy, the

11

same for episcopal conferences as for councils. The first of these is the existence of the college as such. I do not want to stress this too much; we shall certainly have occasion to return to it later.

Then, as you put it very well in your question, there is also the essential conciliarity of the Church. For while it may not be essential for the Church to hold councils, which are particular events, it is essential for it to be conciliar. And in this respect I think that the Russian translation of the word 'catholic' in the creed by *sobornaïa* (= conciliar) is not inaccurate if properly understood. 'Conciliar' basically means 'collegial', as I myself indicated in my book *Towards a Theology of the Laity*, specifically in connection with the Orthodox theology of *sobornost*. 'Conciliar' means both 'synodical' and 'collegial' simultaneously. I suggested that *sobornost* should be translated 'collegial'. I remembered that from the years when I did Russian as a prisoner, and I did a good deal of it; I even ended up having a conversation in Russian, but now, more than forty years later, I've forgotten it all. But I recall that *sobor*, *sobirat* is a Russian verb which means something like 'collect'. One of the sentences always used in grammars is: 'I've been in the forest to collect mushrooms' (*sobirat griby*).

So there is a basis for episcopal conferences, as there is for councils, and that seems to me to be extremely important. Moreover, I once took part in the meeting of the bishops of the French Episcopal Conference at Lourdes, which always takees place about the time of All Saints. Now since I have made a thorough study of the mediaeval councils, on which there are a great many monographs, I am quite certain that in the Middle Ages no one would have hesitated for a second in calling this meeting at Lourdes a council. In fact the bishops first of all meet there to worship: they celebrate together every day, they say the office together – a liturgical dimension is essential to a council – and finally they decide. I was involved in the process of decision. We are told that episcopal conferences are no more than practical organizations, that they have no power of decision and even that they are detrimental to the personal responsibility of bishops. That reminds me rather of a personal intervention by Cardinal

Frings at the Council (since the Cardinal was blind, he needed help in preparing it, and Ratzinger was his theologian and personal adviser). He raised this difficulty. Monsignor Lefebvre was not the only one to object that the decisions of the conference would reduce the personal responsibility of the bishop. Cardinal Gouyon also did so. However, it would be wrong to say that the bishops are not bound by any of the decisions of the episcopal conference. There are at least a number of cases where they are indeed bound by them. The first of these seems to me to be almost too obvious to be worth mentioning: where there is a unanimous vote. Obviously, if the vote is unanimous, each individual is involved and cannot disrupt the solidarity. But there are also other instances. The Jesuit canon lawyer Fr Dortel-Claudot has shown clearly that this is particularly the case when the Roman authorities themselves ask the episcopal conference how a measure envisaged for the universal Church is to be applied. This happened over the question of receiving communion in the hand: the decision on that was left to episcopal conferences and there were episcopal conferences in which it was not accepted, for example in Italy. In France, receiving communion in the hand is accepted and both forms of communion are practised, almost equally and regardless of age. According to Fr Dortel-Claudot there are twenty-seven cases in which canon law itself provides that a Roman decision should be applied by an episcopal conference. In this case the decision is made on a majority vote. Generally there is a more than comfortable majority, well above the famous two-thirds majority which was the majority called for at the Council on all questions of doctrine, while a simple majority is sufficient for practical questions. But generally the majority is well beyond that, and though two or three or four or five bishops may not agree with the decision, they are nevertheless bound by it.

Vatican II recorded and justified a much less rigorous interpretation of the famous saying 'Outside the Church there is no salvation'. Is it right to follow some people in saying that this 'broadening' has led to a devaluation of Christian salvation, a lapse from the specific mission

13

of the Church and a religious relativism, as if all religions were valid as ways to God? What, in your view, is the present task of theology, demonstrating the uniqueness of Christianity as a religion of salvation in a more satisfactory way, without falling into Christian imperialism or maintaining naive claims to universality?

I worked on two conciliar texts on this question, *Lumen Gentium* no.17 and no.7 of the *Decree on the Missionary Activity of the Church*. Taking part in this commission on missions was one of the great blessings of my life. However, there were those on it – I remember one person in particular very clearly, an Indian bishop, Mgr D'Souza – who held purely and simply to the need of baptism for salvation, and that is quite impossible. In fact, even in so important a chapter as that on the need for mission, it is said that God saves by ways which are known to him. We deliberately chose quite a vague formula, without being more specific about the means, since this is a subject on which Catholic theologians do not agree. I once held the theory of implicit faith, for which moreover I could find good authority, notably the text from the Holy Office in the Feeney case, which arose in the United States in 1947 or 1948, but this position has been criticized, in particular by my colleague and friend Fr Liégé. His position was more bound up with eschatology: God will recompense each and every one on the basis of what he or she has done and what he or she has received. And there is also the well-known solution of the anonymous Christian put forward by Karl Rahner (which is often misunderstood). I say that it is misunderstood, since in the context of his work it is in fact bound up with what he calls his transcendental anthropology. That is his own personal view, which is open to criticism, and has not found much acceptance among us.

You asked me what has been the effect of this kind of renunciation of the principle 'Outside the Church there is no salvation', which was put forward, almost simultaneously, around AD 250, by St Cyprian at one end of the Mediterranean and Origen in Alexandria at the other. Does it have consequences for mission?

It is a fact that missions have been in a state of crisis since Vatican II. But to tell the truth, they were already in crisis before the Council and it is for that quite specific reason that the commission on missions at the Council was so dominated by the missionary congregations. At that time, they were suffering from a lack of vocations and no longer had the verve they once had. So if there is a crisis, it goes back further. However, without doubt there has been a consistent crisis, sometimes a very severe one. Some people have gone so far as to say that we do not have to convert others; we simply have to help a Moslem to become a better Moslem, a Hindu to become a better Hindu and so on. That is rather a defeatist reply.

But there has been quite a positive response in the West and also in India. This sees religions as an ordinary way of salvation and Christianity as an extraordinary way. This positive response has been welcomed, and it is advocated by a number of theologians, including – for example – Hans Küng.

I have my own personal position on this matter. Perhaps it is rather complicated to explain, but I would like at least to give a brief summary of it. I was led to re-read books and articles on the question before giving a lecture at the Ecumenical Institute at Tantur (between Jerusalem and Bethlehem) where I spent three months holding a seminar. I was speaking in a country in which non-Christian religions – Judaism and Islam – were dominant, and I spoke of non-biblical religions, at least in the title of my work. Instead of considering the question of religions as such I suggested that we should first look at the individuals who are themselves clearly bound up with a culture and a religion (the one often being connected with the other, and vice versa). Now it is clear that for individuals, the culture in which they live and the religion associated with it are the ordinary ways of salvation, in the sense that 'ordinary' usually has in almost all cases. The exception might perhaps be where 'ordinary' amounted to a theoretical justification of an objective way of salvation represented by religions as such.

At all events, whatever position one holds it is inseparable from the dialogue which is characteristic of the Council and the

Church which has emerged from the Council. The Church is the Church which held the Council and continues to live by it. A dialogue means that the others taking part in it are not just passive. At one time our view of these others could be summed up in the words of the psalm, 'They were in the darkness of death': the missionary came, brought light and all was well. That is too simplistic! Certainly the missionary does bring a light, but we have also to accept from the traditions of those to whom we come what can be integrated into our tradition – that, moreover, is what the Council texts say – and that takes a good deal of time, of patience. Much needs to be worked out, and there has to be a work of discernment between what is valuable and possible and what is not. You might see a kind of outline plan for all this, if one cares to put it that way, in the address which John-Paul II gave to 80,000 young people in the great Mohammed V Stadium in Casablanca. In fact he affirmed the possibility of dialogue very strongly. He pronounced the name of Jesus Christ just once: I have to say that there is quite a deep difference between us there. But he added that a good deal of light still had to be cast on this difference. In short, it was very positive.

Beyond question, we must still proclaim Jesus Christ. In the conciliar *Declaration on Non-Christian Religions* there is a passage which says this very well. It was composed on the insistence of Fr Daniélou, but of course with unanimous support. To proclaim Jesus Christ it is not always necessary to speak of him or to preach him explicitly. Suppose we take the example which was given in the commission on missions at the Council, that of the White Fathers or the sisters who still remain in Algeria, a country which is clearly no longer what it was from a Catholic point of view. Now many of these sisters and possibly these White Fathers are not even at the head of Christian communities; perhaps they are doing social work or teaching in state institutions. Someone suggested that this might be described as pre-evangelization, but we said no. It is already evangelization from the moment the sign is introduced, albeit in quite a tacit way; people are very well aware that these are priests or religious.

16

So the preaching of Christ is not necessarily verbal preaching, though it is desirable that it should eventually turn into that. We are far too well aware, particularly in France, of a kind of ideal Christianity in which the masses were thought to belong to the Church. Clearly we are increasingly aware that we are a minority, at least in terms of practising faithful. But we still retain something of the idea, an obsession with the masses, whereas I shall have occasion to make some comments here in favour of individuals, of small groups. In this connection I am extremely impressed when I hear of Protestants who deal only with small groups: a pastor may perhaps go thirty or forty miles to meet a family or three people. I admire these people very much and I think that there are great depths to them. So I am all for action involving small groups and on a small scale. But at the same time – and this goes with what I have just said – we cannot forget activity through the media, which at present have enormous influence. We might recall the Pope's travels here. The Nuncio, Mgr Felici, once visited me here in my hospital room and I expressed some reservations about the Holy Father's journeys: he may be confronted with an audience of several hundred thousand people, but what is left afterwards? I did, though, also pass on what some Africans had said to me: 'What the Holy Father leaves behind among us is pride in being African, pride in being Catholic. He has brought us that pride, and that is no small thing if it is properly understood.' But the Nuncio said to me: 'You should remember that when the Pope has an audience of a million, as he did in Colombia, he does more in an hour or two than a missionary does in fifteen years.' Yes and no, I would say. But in some ways yes. So the effect of the media is also important alongside the effect of small-scale activity on the individual and the small group. When it comes to communication, John-Paul II is the world Number One: he has an amazing gift of presence and the media run after him.

I have just made a rather dogmatic pronouncement on the question I was asked. Speaking dogmatically, and that is more than theology, Jesus Christ is the absolute and unsurpassable religion in the sense that if there are intelligent beings on other

17

planets than ours – and after all that is possible – while these beings would not have Jesus as saviour, they would have him as Lord, as King, as the criterion of any possible relationship with God. From the moment when Jesus is God-man in a single person according to a unity of which there is no higher example, it is evident that he is the absolute religion, the fullness and the perfect example of the religious relationship. And he is that not by the exclusion of other factors, possibly other religions, but by inclusion. The perspective is changed a great deal when it is inclusive and not exclusive.

That having been said, let me add an idea of which I am very fond but which I have not been able to develop as I should. At one time I collected together some notes on it, but all that is now a long way in the past. The idea is the notion of 'firstfruits'. When we see, for example, St Paul saying, 'Achaea has heard the word of God', what does Achaea represent? Not all the population, but perhaps a few hundred faithful. It was a small group, but a small representative group. I am a firm believer in the biblical idea of 'one for many', an idea which Cullmann has developed in his numerous biblical studies, showing how the history of humanity comes to be concentrated little by little in one individual, Jesus Christ, and then expands again after him. So I think that the minorities, the small groups, could have this role of representing a totality which they mysteriously bring towards God ('by ways which God knows', as the Council says).

Clearly all that I have just said should be completed by a study on the meaning of salvation. People often talk about it: 'religions of salvation', 'Christ the Saviour' and so on. But there are very few studies on the topic. The new theological development is only just beginning. The Catholic idea of salvation takes in all creation. Péguy said: 'I would put into heaven whatever has succeeded.' I think that there is some truth to his comment and it makes a great impression on me that each year the liturgy makes Lent, the preparation for Easter, begin with the story of the creation. And it takes it up again on Easter Eve. It is because there is a first creation that there is a second creation. It is because there is creation that there is redemption and that redemption takes in the whole of creation.

There is an extremely important insight here: in reality the creation is already taken up into the paschal mystery towards which it ascends. So I too would put in my heaven whatever has succeeded.

In this perspective should we not remind ourselves that the preparation for the kingdom of God does not go exclusively through the Church?

Clearly the Church is a preparation for the kingdom. But it is not the only preparation. The wider world, the lay world and the other religions, is also a preparation for the kingdom. And that is very important. I recall a very fine passage in which Moltmann applies this idea to Judaism. There is a question which we do not ask often enough and which the most recent Roman document on Judaism in particular has scarcely developed, the question of the value of Judaism as the root of Christianity: Mary, Jesus and all the apostles were Jews. It's easy enough to stop there. That was said in 1985. Since then the Roman authorities have spoken in a positive way not only of a Judaism which is still alive and active, which has a meaning before God, but also of the bond between the Jewish people and the land of Israel. I am thinking of John Paul II's apostolic letter for Good Friday 1984, and above all of the notes dated 24 June 1985 which were published by the Secretariat for Unity presided over by Cardinal Willebrands (*Istina*, June 1986). I know that the Jews said that they were disappointed with the text: they had expected something more, something better. The fact remains that we can rejoice at the progress which has been achieved and that this progress heralds yet further progress. Judaism is alive. It has an extraordinarily developed and profound thought. There is a religious life in Judaism, a life of worship and witness, of sanctification of the name. In reality, as Moltmann says, in that way Judaism is also a preparation for the kingdom.

Beyond Judaism, and in a way which is still not clear to us, we should also consider Islam, the other religions, lay people themselves. Indeed it can rightly be said that sometimes the laity have done more than we have. I recall a remark by Evdokimov to the effect that 'Those who have the message of liberation are not the same as those who actually liberate.' Certainly things often seem to happen like that. We are the repository of the message of liberation, but sometimes it is others who liberate. All that must be taken into account in the idea of the relationship between the Church and the kingdom and therefore also in the idea of salvation.

But I would like to return to the idea of salvation, because I am aware that all that I have said about it is in terms of the final aspect of the fulfilment of the (first) creation. That is true, but it does not indicate the evil that has to be overcome. I like the two illustrations that Fr de Lubac chose for his book *Catholicism*: the bearing of the cross and the Pentecost from the tympanum of Vézelay, with the comment that the one was the condition of the other. Yes, there is evil which must be overcome before the success of the kingdom is achieved. And for that we need the help of a redeemer. Vladimir Soloviev opened the preface to the philosophical testament which he wrote in 1899 with these words: 'Is evil only a natural deficiency, an absence of fulfilment which disappears of its own accord with the growth of good, or is it an effective force which, by employing seductions, dominates our world in such a way that if we are to struggle against it and win, we need support in another order of existence?' I wrote on my ordination picture (which depicts St Dominic at the foot of the cross) two lines which I think are by Tennyson:

But none of the ransomed ever knew
How deep were the waters crossed.

This is clearly an allusion to the liberation of the Israelites from Egypt by their crossing of the Red Sea. We also talk of ransom, and we talk of the redeemer. 'Someone paid the price of your redemption', writes St Paul (I Corinthians 6.20). But the most decisive text is Mark 10.45: 'The Son of Man came to... give his life a ransom for many.' The words 'for many' reappear in Matthew 26.28 and Mark 14.24 in connection with the blood of the covenant of which our eucharist is the memorial or sacramental realization. The Old Testament has quite a large number of terms to denote redemption, ransom, but two are important: *gaal*, of which the active participle is *goel*, and *padah*. However, the contexts in which these terms are used or applied are different: *padah* comes from commercial law, and *gaal/goel* from family law: a kinsman is the *goel* of a member of his family when he restores his or her rights by paying a debt, as Boaz did for Ruth.

What does Jesus give as a ransom? His life. And to whom does he give it? To the multitude, to us. So he is our *goel*, he establishes us as members of the family of God; his blood is that of the covenant (new, eternal). And how does he achieve that? By his death and his resurrection through which, in taking their sins upon himself, he restores all men and women to be members of the family of God, in him, the one who is the Son and heir. The salvation thus acquired is applied to many people who know neither Christ nor God, by ways that God knows. For those of us who have received the gospel, if we welcome it in faith, salvation comes through baptism and eucharist, sacraments of his death and resurrection. By them we become members of the body of Christ, co-heirs. We make his life ours, given for us, to us.

I am aware that I am stammering, and stammering very badly; theology is too profound a mystery, but that is the direction in which I would like to go.

– 2 –

Do We Know Christianity?

You have spent all your life working for a better understanding of Christianity and in particular for reconciliation among the Christian Churches. However, do we not have to take note of the enormous gulf that has opened up between specialist research and religious knowledge among the majority of people?

For example, most people, and not only the young, no longer have any idea about what would be regarded as a common foundation of Western Christian culture; words like gospel, Trinity, sacraments, Good Friday, Easter, All Saints, not to mention parish, bishops, etc., no longer mean anything. What do you as a theologian think of this situation?

Does not this state of affairs, beyond theology, put in question the approach of part of our culture: is Europe conceivable without Christianity?

In France, the 1985 Vivien Report on the sects, for all its limitations, puts in question the French ideology of the laity 'which has been transformed so that it is ignorant of and neutral towards the reflection and the teaching of the great philosophical trends and religions of the world, in which France has a place'.

Does proper religious instruction at school seem to you to be desirable?

Let me take the first three questions together. One can only tackle them in a specific, historical fashion. And those of us who are French Catholics find that our history both sustains us and somewhat stifles us.

Europe and secularization

Europe was made by Christianity. It is impossible to see modern Europe without Christianity. When people talk about immigrants, they sometimes say that France has been made by many races (Roman, Celtic, Germanic and so on). I have even heard it said in Parliament, and it is true. But at the time these races were integrated into a very strong structure, which was that of the Church, and in those days the Roman Catholic Church. Nowadays when people talk about a multi-racial, multi-cultural society, with a kind of acceptance of everything, no matter what, including a Moslem culture which is alien to us, and so on, into what do they want to integrate all this and what force is to produce the integration? Social laws? That will not be enough. What is needed is integration by a spiritual force. One might have to resort to those secularized Christian values which we shall have to talk about in due course. But in my view they will not be enough, since Europe was made not only by Christianity but also – though this may surprise you – by monasticism. When Paul VI named St Benedict the patron saint of Europe I think that he had a very profound intuition, since it was really monasticism, and in particular the Benedictine order, which deeply shaped Europe.

But this Christianity and this monasticism have been monopolized by the Church, and by a Church which became increasingly clerical and even ended up by being very theocratic and even hierocratic (theocracy being the domination of God and hierocracy the domination of priests). That was very serious, because it provoked a reaction: I would like to call it a reaction of empirical common sense against a supposedly 'supernatural' explanation. It was ridiculous to explain an invasion of rats by saying that people had not been going to mass. And it was ridiculous to explain a sickness as being a consequence of blasphemy, because in reality there are secondary causes, real causes, specific causes. So at a particular moment in every realm of life those knowledgeable in the world of human realities rebelled against the claim of the clergy and above all the

23

senior hierarchy that they had a right to dominate and control everything and ultimately to stifle research into earthly truths. The process of secularization, which asserted itself with science at the end of the sixteenth century, was able to reinforce a process of declericalization which had preceded it (from the Middle Ages on) and which was accentuated by the secularization of politics in the nineteenth century. (The whole mediaeval period is full of struggles between the priesthood and the empire – or the priesthood and the monarchies.)

Granted, questions could be asked here, since we are experiencing instances of the return of religious totalitarianism: one might think of Iran today. What is called Moslem fundamentalism is ultimately very important in the contemporary world. Then there were other spheres. After politics, during the Middle Ages, there was culture. Humanism, which at first was essentially religious – Lucien Febvre's book on Rabelais shows clearly how unthinkable atheism was at that period – changed direction and became lay humanism (in France that happened with Montaigne). But again, Montaigne was a good Catholic, who made a pilgrimage to Loreto, and so on.

After culture came lay ethics. Here one might take as an example Voltaire in the Calas affair, or in the affair of the Chevalier de la Barre, or Voltaire accusing providence after the Lisbon earthquake. In short, a lay ethic emerged to contest a clerical ethic which claimed universal dominance and offered a 'supernatural' explanation for everything which was really in the hands of the priests. The process continued in the nineteenth century with the laicization of history (for example with Jules Michelet) and with science (which produced scientism).

In this way the meaning of the word 'lay' came to be changed completely. Whereas 'lay' used to denote simply a member of the Church who has not been ordained – that is still what 'lay' means when used of Christians – it has come to mean 'anticlerical', alien to a doubtful supernaturalism. This has given rise to a lay world in the modern sense of the world, which is a complete world. This change is very important. I am most impressed by the way in which people with moral integrity lead

24

lives which are filled entirely with not only the benefits but also the very heavy obligations of modern life, without any other concerns. As we sing in a hymn, *Nihil perenne cogitat* ('He no longer thinks of the eternal'). Obviously this secularization of life indubitably includes the laicization of a large number of Christian values. One might recall the short book by M.de Certeau and J.M.Domenach, *Le Christianisme éclaté*: the explosion of Christianity into a host of values like brotherhood (socialism as we have it today), justice, peace, tolerance, a whole host of values which have become independent of Christianity and have sometimes come to be opposed to it. For unfortunately the clergy have become hardened in their theocracy and are *a priori* opposed to all this.

This laicization raises serious questions for us, because of a certain gulf between Christianity and the rest of human life. Christianity has become purely a private matter, though this is quite relative, since the Church still has a great many public roles, and there are links between it and the secular world. But on the whole there is no doubt that we have a 'complete' society which offers all the means for leading an earthly life that is at the same time both difficult and pleasant, and which leaves religion solely to the personal conscience of individuals, at least until a serious crisis makes us aware of the fragility of our plans.

You have alluded to the problems of the laity, which have already been indicated in connection with the Vivien Report. What would you like to say about that report?

The Vivien Report contains the extremely interesting idea that an 'open laicity' should replace an exclusive laicity. But we must be careful about generalizations. I have visited the lay school and there weren't many problems there. Just once, perhaps, when a teacher referred to a *Life of Jesus* which was that of Renan, but this was in no way an attack: quite the contrary.

I would compare the Vivien Report with an article which I noted at the time, written by the Protestant professor Roger Mehl. It appeared in *Le Monde* and took very much the same line. He spoke of a new vision of the laity which was not exclusively ideological but specific; in other words it included the reality of France today. Now there is not the least doubt that France was created by Christianity, particularly by the Catholic Church – I would add, the Roman Catholic Church: the link between France and Rome is extremely deep. I recall, too, how after the suppression of the Faculty of Theology at the Sorbonne, when Section V of the École Pratique des Hautes Études was created in 1886, a statement was made to the Chamber of Deputies that there are things in theological teaching which, renewed in accordance with the demands of science, 'should not disappear completely from all teaching in our country'.

That clearly presupposes much that has yet to be achieved, but that is rather the object of a brotherly struggle, namely peace in the schools (we are moving in that direction), some change in the overall climate of the teacher training colleges, and from our side a dialogue started by the Church.

Does the development of the catechism seem to you to be a good one?

First of all I should tell you that I do not think myself very competent to speak about that, although I consider the question to be an extremely important one. It is impossible to do everything, and I have never myself taught the catechism or worked in that area. However, I have followed some of the discussion, and I listen regularly on Radio Notre-Dame, at least once if not twice a week, to the programme by the director of catechetics, which provides some very interesting information.

First I should say that I fully approve the plan behind current work on catechesis and the catechism, namely that it should follow the development of children, their vocabulary and what they can understand. These are things of which we are very aware today, thanks to the work of Piaget and many others, whereas once not much account was taken of them: the child was thought of as an incomplete adult, and indeed was often regarded in a very negative way. Today people tend to go to the opposite extreme, as though all children were brilliant! It is true

26

that children have quite amazing resources, but obviously these have to undergo development. So the intention is excellent. Has it been realized? That remains to be seen, and I cannot comment.

Clearly we always have to teach, even the child of eight, nine or ten, who is very receptive from the religious point of view, even mystical. Children often have amazing intuitions and very deep capacities for understanding. Beyond question we must teach. But on the other hand, if one takes the old catechism as a model (I certainly studied it and was even the first in the class to learn the printed replies off by heart), I would nevertheless ask: 'How much sticks?' There are those who have said (the philosopher Étienne Gilson was among them), 'I remember my catechism as though it were yesterday', but that is exceptional. Most of the time, not much sticks. And it cannot be said that in its old form the catechism was so successful that one should follow its line exactly.

In the more immediate present this question comes up in connection with *Pierres vivantes*, a textbook which has provoked a great many debates. There has been systematic criticism of this book by people who are not all fundamentalist but quite simply conservative or worried about the way things are going. I personally did not agree from the start with the way in which the book opens, beginning with Moses and not with Genesis. Granted, from the critical point of view the first texts come from the ninth century BC and the stories of the creation and the flood are not historically prior to them. But from an educational point of view I think that one has to get over this difficulty and that one should really follow the order of events in the text, even if that means giving a warning at some point that in terms of the historical origins of the text the order is different. Moreover you will know that the book has now been revised and expanded; there are about forty or fifty new entries in the table of contents, so that it risks having become rather too full or complicated. However, this is not the children's catechism; it is the 'teacher's book'. On the other hand we have 220,000 catechists in France, which is quite splendid, one of the strengths of which the Church today can be proud, though I ask myself whether all these men

27

and women have really been trained for the task that they are taking on. Still, this reservation relates to particular cases and does not affect the principle, which is excellent.

Does that not raise the question of the enormous distance which separates 'academic theology' and the religious knowledge of 'ordinary' Christians, if one can put it that way? And is there not, at any rate in France, a neglected link in the transmission of the faith, that of catechetics for adults, and not just for catechists who themselves should rightly make a personal effort at reflection and training?

It is true that in France we do not have any middle ground between scholarly research, which is scientific or somewhat technical, and popularization in the good sense of the word. However, there are people involved in popularization. For despite everything, in France we have a Catholic press which is of very great value: the publications of Bayard Presse and *La Croix*, *La Vie*, Fleurus, *Panorama aujourd'hui*, *Fêtes et Saisons*, and so on. But there is often nothing in between. For this is not something for a theologian to do: indeed, he or she may be incapable of doing it. I recently tried to write a book on the Holy Spirit at the request of a friend who wanted something more accessible than my three-volume *I Believe in the Holy Spirit*. It was called *Spirit of Man, Spirit of God*, but that is another task.

Do you think that there are enough resources in France for the training of young theologians?

I think that a great many things do not get done in France for lack of resources. In this respect the poverty of the Church is real and very profound. Or the resources that the Church has – and she still has some – are invested in plant rather than being in a liquid form and capable of being used immediately. In Germany, outside the universities I see the academies. Moreover I have stayed in them, and spoken in the Munich academy. However, we seem incapable of doing anything of this kind.

Nevertheless, in the dioceses, and sometimes even within the very buildings of the major seminaries, there are institutions for training people, above all the laity. And as for more technical theology, we have our Catholic Institutes and our faculties of theology, and they are not doing too badly. Clearly the general lack of vocations – in the sense of vocations to the priesthood – is a very serious matter. A bishop who ordains one priest every two years and who nevertheless makes the effort of sending one of his seminarians or one of his young priests for training in a university or an institute is almost heroic. At the Catholic Institute in Paris, where on several occasions I took part in meetings of doctoral students, above all with Fr Geffré, first of all I was very struck by the very fine quality and the variety of the topics that they had chosen, and then I noticed that these doctorands were by no means all seminarians or young priests with no other work to do, but often priests with one or two important responsibilities in a diocese, like post-ordination training or acting as chaplain to various branches of Catholic Action, and so on. In other words, those who were doing this technical work were of very fine quality and far above the usual level.

Finally, I would say that the training provided is certainly very inadequate, but it is not negative or catastrophic. One might consider the list of doctoral topics published each year. Moreover, when it comes to liturgy, those who take liturgy seriously in Spain, the United States and Canada will have been at the Liturgical Institute in Paris. I even recall that when I was sent by the Ministry of Cultural Affairs to Spain to give lectures in various institutes or universities, I wrote a report with the warm recommendation that two or three bursaries should be created each year for foreign students at the Liturgical Institute. I could give other examples.

Once lay theologians have finished their training course, can they find suitable work?

Often lay people who do theology do not intend to teach theology or to continue technical study of it, but rather to deepen their

29

own education, frequently with a view to teaching children or doing catechetics. But it is true that it is rare for the theological training of laity to end up in a paid job and that the Church ought to be concerned about this. In fact there are very few openings in theological teaching for the laity, and the important posts often remain closed to them.

On what points should theological research be focussed today?

I can only give an incomplete answer to this question. Who is up to dealing with it? However, I would put in first place the first article of the creed: 'God the Creator'. It seems to me extremely important to be aware that it is the lack of a precise understanding of creation which prevents people from believing seriously in the second creation. We must accept that it is not easy to believe truly in the second creation, in a new world, what is sometimes called the 'kingdom of God', a new heaven and a new earth, as a result of the resurrection of Jesus. One can truly believe that if one already believes in a first creation which is more a kind of sketch, a very precarious sketch in expectation of something else, which is redemption or the salvation that I mentioned earlier. Moreover, this point seems to me to be extremely important if we are to take the problem of evil seriously, and that is a problem which troubles a great many people or prevents them from becoming believers.

The first creation is no more than a sketch, awaiting further development. In this connection I am very fond of Claudel's comment: 'The problem was so enormous that only the Word could respond to it, bringing not an explanation but a presence.' This is a presence which is not that of an object, but an active presence of hope, finally that of the resurrection. However, while this reply may be valid for us, it cannot convince anyone for whom the problem of evil is an absolute obstacle. This question of God the Creator also seems to me to be very important for the basis of ethics. Otherwise, human beings are surrendered to their autonomous power of self-creation; they take their power to transform things as being a real creation. The result of that in the sphere of sexuality, freedom and so on is a tendency to escape the rules of faith. Unfortunately, though, it has to be said that these rules were often resolutions imposed by the clerical Church authorities, rather than criteria for regulating faith.

After God the Creator, anthropology would seem to me to pose another problem. I would not see it only in theoretical terms, as the study of human beings in their structures (and in this connection the human sciences have a major contribution to offer, as does philosophical reflection), but also in a historical approach, in particular through the Bible. It seems to me that in the Bible, which is a history orientated from a beginning to an end, there is a consistent contribution to an understanding of human nature. Progressively we are shown our possibilities, our limits, our conditioning. There again anthropology ends up in ethics: it conditions a great many reflections which are constantly changing – and necessarily so – since we now know more than we used to, for example in the time of Alphonsus Liguori. I would also put in this context the very important question of the role of the woman: the woman is also self-creative, strongly conditioned by her vocation to motherhood, even if she does not exercise it, and by her relationship to the man.

In third place (though without rating it less important, since I am concerned here with the whole of the theological enterprise) I would put the need to be open to the profound values of others, of all the others, and most particularly of the confessions or Christian Churches. So I have made a fairly thorough study of Orthodoxy, Protestantism, Luther; here – and I would also add in Wesley, the Methodists and the Baptists – there are depths which we have not investigated among ourselves, which we have yet to realize.

That was, in fact, my argument in *Chrétiens désunis*, in 1937. It was not very welcome to Rome at the time because I said that we also had to accept others, and in those days that was hardly recognized. In fact this insight is not sufficiently implemented even today, though it has been accepted in principle since the Council. We are often left with a kind of peaceful co-existence:

31

we are friends, we visit one another as if we were going to a kind of second, weekend home, but that is not enough. The whole of theology must be penetrated by this dialogue: the Trinity, the Church, ministers, the sacraments, the Virgin Mary, anthropology, ethics...

I would like to stress a new, original reflection which amounts to a real creation – one that is truly unprecedented – about the real and original character of law in the Church.

Canon Law (*Codex juris canonici*) was drawn up in 1917 – and the Pope promulgated a new edition of it in January 1983 – on the model of the constitutional authors of the eighteenth century. Pottmeyer has even shown that Vatican I pursued the power and indeed the idea of sovereignty to be found in the philosophy of either Bodin (in France) or Hobbes (in England), which are alien to the Christian tradition of the true and original nature of law in the Church. Nowadays people have begun to reflect on the subject, but there are not many books. I would simply call attention to a very interesting article by my colleague and friend H.Legrand in the book entitled *L'Église: Institution et Foi*, produced by the Faculté Saint-Louis in Brussels in 1979, and above all the very fine piece by Corecco in the volume on *La Réception de Vatican II*. It is a very major study, long and detailed, which is a criticism of canon law, even in its new garb, in the name of the originality of canon law. I myself published an article along these lines entitled 'Rudolf Sohm nous interroge encore' (Rudolf Sohm still has questions for us), in which, after pointing out the major criticisms made by Sohm, I showed how profound the question was and how we could reply along lines which met up to some degree with his researches: there is a Christian ontology with a sacramental basis, but this then needs to be made more specific by a law. For example, baptism creates the Christian personality in the communion of the Church: it is then necessary to specify the rights and duties of those who have been baptized. The same is true of marriage, and the degrees of Church order. At this point I join company with the formula of a lay theologian of the nineteenth century, Pilgram, who in 1860 published a book in which he demonstrated that the Church is a *koinonia* in the form of a *politeia*, a 'communion' in the form of a 'society'. In other words, the Church is a communion with a sacramental basis which is therefore supernatural, but which specifies the ways in which it is to be implemented and its social form, i.e. a form with a law. That is a sphere which remains to be investigated.

– 3 –

The Religions

Islam

What do you think of Islam?

The theological status of Islam is an immense problem that I haven't really studied. There was, for example, the position of Massignon, for whom it was a heresy of Judaeo-Christianity. For Fr Daniélou Islam was a regression towards the faith of Abraham, and I quite like this position, without regarding it in any pejorative way, for the positive side of Islam as a religion is indisputable.

Is Mohammed an inspired prophet? I think that one can accept that, not in the sense of full biblical inspiration, but in the sense in which many religious men are inspired. Beyond question Mohammed was an extremely great and extremely profound religious figure.

What are the positive values of Islam? What is the source of the power of Islam which is so manifest today, since Islam is growing rather than diminishing: in Africa, Asia, Indonesia...? It is an immense realm, from the Pacific islands to the Atlantic. The first quality of Islam is simplicity. In Islam there is only one dogma: God is God, God is omnipotent and, they add, Mohammed is his prophet. That is an extremely powerful affirmation of pure transcendence, compared with which Christian faith – and above all Catholic faith – is quite certainly a complicated matter. As we know, when one adds the Trinity, the Incarnation, the sacraments, things become very complex.

Hence, first of all, the simplicity of the pure transcendence of God. In the Koran there are ninety-nine names for God: the conqueror, the merciful, the sublime, and so on; the hundredth God has reserved for himself: it is a sign of transcendence and simplicity. Another value is that Islam embraces the whole of life. We are very well aware that it is not just a religion but politics, a social framework of brotherhood, and a very real brotherhood at that.

There remains the problem of the relationship of Islam to modern life. At El Elazar in Cairo efforts were made at adaptation, but these were soon opposed by the Moslem Brothers. In fact Islam is itself resistance to modernity: we obviously have a supreme example of this in the case of Khomeini in Iran, since his revolution is essentially anti-Western, anti-modern.

I myself had quite an interesting experience of this when I was at Tantur, the ecumenical institute near Jerusalem. I went with some friends to a Koran school at Hebron. There we found boys and girls, playing, all dressed in a kind of blue uniform. However, they did not mix. They welcomed us with great joy because we were proof that they had not been abandoned, that Europeans were thinking of Palestine. Then we had a meeting with men of some standing, as it were judges, and I well remember asking them about the historical attitude of Islam. They replied vaguely with quotations from the Koran: a divine book, which had fallen just as it was from heaven, and which no one could touch – in principle it should not even be translated, since it was divine, even down to its language. I noted that this resistance to modernity had an extremely deep foundation from the Islamic point of view. But again, there are some openings and that is absolutely necessary. The opposite would be impossible.

The third value of Islam that I would stress would be mysticism. This is not only profound but widely represented – there are famous Moslem mystics like al-Hallaj, who was studied by Massignon (I was present when he was defending his thesis one Wednesday, the eve of Ascension Day: he referred to that festival), but there are many others, for example Ibn Arabi, and yet others whom I barely know personally. However, I recall a meeting, again at Tantur, with American friends connected with a Moslem boy, paralysed and very deeply religious: together we spoke of Moslem prayer, which arrives at a real friendship with God.

Islam has all those values.

I do not think that it has a great religious influence in France; perhaps not enough – I don't know.

Do you think that it is legitimate to allow a church to be turned into a mosque?

Obviously that pains me. But in France at present there are at least three million Moslem workers, often with their families. At the Invalides I myself have had a Moslem nurse, actually born in France, though all her family is at Constantine. That's a fact. But I truly think that France, which is Christian, cannot open itself up to Islam. At all events, since that is the situation – at least three million, that's something, with families sometimes settled here for two or three generations – in these conditions, at a strictly pastoral level, there is not only a necessity but perhaps even a duty or at least very good reason, to give them the possibility of remaining believers, of praying, if there is church that is no longer of any use to anyone. As I say, it does not give me any pleasure, but I have to admit it.

Judaism

There is a growing interest among Christians in Judaism. How do you explain it?

I explain it first of all by a certain feeling, that of having to redeem ourselves. Jules Isaac spoke of a degree of Christian responsibility for modern antisemitism which, as we know, ended up in genocide, the 'holocaust', or rather the *shoah*, the great trial, since six million Jews were exterminated by the Nazis. Clearly the Nazis did not have any Christian point of reference: Hitler was baptized and a Catholic in his childhood, but there was absolutely nothing Catholic about him, nor did he have a Catholic faith. So this responsibility is very indirect, but we can hardly say that it is not there, and we do indeed have to redeem ourselves. That is the first theme, more or less conscious, but nevertheless real.

Then, at least for those who are aware of it, there is the manifest renewal of the vitality of Judaism, which can itself be explained by the holocaust and the creation of Israel as an independent Jewish state (from the Jewish point of view this is extremely important, and the adoption of Jerusalem as the capital is very profound). Granted, it is not accepted by all the powers, nor by the Vatican, but if I were a Jew I would regard that as the apple of my eye: it's so important! But there is more; there is the greatness of a people which has the Bible as its history and the psalms as its prayer. There is undoubtedly a renewal of Jewish thought which goes very deep. Few among us are aware of it. I myself am not sufficiently aware of it, but one does what one can, and the little that I do know is very remarkable. I was able to make the acquaintance of people like Martin Buber, whom I once met when I was at the École Biblique and went into Jewish Jerusalem; André Néher, whom I knew quite well at Strasbourg and who is now at Jerusalem; and finally Abraham Heschel, several of whose works I read before meeting him. I said to myself: 'If I meet that man one day, I'll kiss him.' I did meet him; he had a beard and I said to him: 'Look, despite your beard I'm going to kiss you, because what you have written is very fine and very profound.' This Jewish thought can add much to our understanding of the Bible, God and humanity. I also met Gershom Scholem in Jerusalem.

I would say above all that one of the great problems for us Christians and Catholics is to attach some meaning to Jewish vitality after Christ, since Judaism is creative even today. I have already referred to the way in which Moltmann gave a rapid reply to this question when he said that the Church did not only have to prepare for the kingdom of God. The religions, the lay world itself, but primarily Israel had a contribution to make to this preparation. I regret that this aspect of things has been treated too gently in the Roman document which appeared several years ago on Judaism. Moreover this document is a step backward in comparison with earlier ones, not only the document produced by the episcopal commission but also the document produced by the Church of Rome (not the Roman Church as the universal Church with Rome as its centre but the Church of Rome, the diocese of Rome, since in Rome there is still the great synagogue which neither the Nazis nor Mussolini destroyed). Moreover, more recent declarations like those which I cited earlier and the visit by John Paul II to the Synagogue of Rome on 13 April 1986 represent progress on this great question: what is the significance of this perennial character of Israel even to the point of eschatology? Clearly I am not embarking on a commentary on Romans 9-11: 'All Israel will be saved.' You know as well as I do the book by my colleague and friend Fr Refoulé, which is very learned, but which has not, I think, found a unanimous following.

From a Christian point of view, can one be happy to accord Judaism the same place as Islam?

The parallelism is not justified. Basically, Islam does not raise internal questions, whereas Judaism confronts us with one. We bear Judaism in our hearts. Islam is external to Christianity, whereas Judaism is internal to it, at least in its roots. Only these roots are inseparable from what followed, because Judaism has continued, and what it has experienced since then also has a message for us.

Are you less concerned with the religions of the Far East?

I know too little about the great religions of the East to speak of them. There was the meeting at Assisi on 17 October 1986 and I think that it will have a sequel. I have only been able to glance at the latest book by Hans Küng. It is more a confrontation than a dialogue. And the recent book on the state of the religions which has just appeared makes us modest about the knowledge that one can have of religions, their complexity and their riches.

— 4 —

The Church

Your work as a theologian has above all been concerned with the Church. Following other Christian theologians and thinkers (from Moehler to Monsieur Portal), but with a tenacity which is all your own, you have made it your life's work. One could say that your work has clearly raised the following question: how does one move from a church conceived above all as a hierarchy (with its Roman centralism and its clericalism) to a church which is a communion and the people of God? The importance of your work can be measured by the magnitude of this task, which seeks to reverse a slow historical trend in the Church from the time of Gregory VII, in the eleventh century, with famous landmarks like the Fourth Lateran Council (1215), and the Councils of Trent and Vatican I, whatever may have been their positive contributions to the history of Christianity. A first question in this connection: do you still think that the eleventh century (and the period which followed it) is a decisive moment in the history of the Roman Catholic Church, with the clergy autonomous over against the secular power, the dissociation of the Church from the eucharist and the first absolute ordinations, the birth of scholastic theology, compulsory celibacy for priests in the Latin Church, the Decretum Gratiani *in the twelfth century, and so on?*

There is no doubt that for me the great turning point in ecclesiology is the eleventh century. That turning point is, of course, embodied in the person of Gregory VII, the anniversary of whose death was celebrated in 1985, and it includes the whole of the Gregorian reform, for Gregory VII set in motion a development which lasted long after his time. In particular he asked the canon lawyers to assemble the largest possible number of texts on pontifical power because he was engaged in a struggle (a very necessary struggle, in which he finally proved victorious) against the control of ecclesiastical posts by laymen (lords, kings and emperors): this was the famous investiture dispute. It very soon proved that the foundation of this reform was the Holy See, Rome, the pontifical power. There had already been somewhat disjointed attempts at reform at the episcopal level, and other forces were involved, in particular the monks and above all Cluny, but finally papal power proved to be the most effective. So the struggle determined the course of research into canon law, during the lifetime of Gregory VII and afterwards, from 1080 down to the first years of the twelfth century; this, moreover, was the period when the question of investitures found its real solution, the solution for the future, which was provided by a fine French canon lawyer, St Yvo of Chartres. He distinguished between two aspects of investiture: on the one hand the lay aspect, if you like to put it that way, the king bestowing the episcopate, in the sense that the word episcopate denoted lands and benefices, and on the other hand spiritual power in the strict sense, which was not given by the lord, king or emperor, but was purely ecclesiastical, clearly depending on the sacraments.

This insight gave a new impetus to the study of canon law – for canon law had existed since the third and the fourth centuries, in particular at the time of Gelasius. This study culminated with the famous *Decretum Gratiani*, which is dated very precisely to 1140, shortly before the middle of the twelfth century; the *Decretum* gave the Church an enormous and often contradictory collection of documents: the exact title is 'Decree on the distinction and the concordance of the canons'. Gratian often quotes mutually contradictory formulae, whether from the Councils or the Popes or possibly even from the Fathers of the Church, under the same heading and in the same chapter. And he was very well aware of this. It has been shown that this procedure provided anyone who had to decide on a particular problem with different ways of exercising his pastoral responsibility, depending on his personal prudence and on circumstances. That is very interesting. Nowadays it is easier for everything to be decided, in particular in the Codex. The *Decretum Gratiani* is not a code, since a code is a modern invention, in imitation of the Napoleonic code which inaugurated the era of codes at the beginning of the nineteenth century. Nor was it any longer a matter of constantly referring to Rome, as had often been the case, and proved one of the great reasons for the development of Roman power. It was not so much that Rome sought to extend its power – though that also happened - as that bishops found it easier to make enquiries of the Holy See, which had good offices, good archives and often gave extremely wise answers; for example the *Decretals* of Innocent III are models of canonical and pastoral wisdom.

But to return to Gregory VII. Papal power, as a truly fundamental axis, an axis or solid foundation for the reform that was needed, ended up by making the Church itself into a legal institution. It did so in several respects. First of all, when the Church opposed the temporal power – which it had been obliged to do for centuries, because it also had temporal claims and the temporal power had spiritual pretensions – it was led to adopt very much the same attitudes as the temporal power itself, to conceive of itself as a society, as a power, when in reality it is a communion, with ministers, servants. Secondly, what led to the Church becoming a legal institution was the affirmation of papal power as the basis of everything. In the famous *Dictatus Papae* – the twenty-seven incredible propositions of Gregory VII, the aim of which is still being discussed – it is said expressly that a simple papal delegate, a simple nuncio, even if he is not a bishop (it often happened that he was a deacon), has authority over bishops, archbishops and all the rest of the Church. That shows how the legal has priority over the sacramental.

This primacy of the legal over the sacramental then reappears to some degree in a terminological development which Fr de Lubac brought out in a definitive way in his famous *Corpus mysticum*, which appeared in 1944. In this work one can see the

42

change in the way in which the terms *corpus Christi* and *corpus mysticum* were applied. Towards the middle of the twelfth century, these terms moved from the eucharist (where they denoted the mystical, sacramental body) to the Church conceived of as a society, to such a degree that 'mystical body' became the equivalent of the Church as a society. That is a very important development, since it contributed to this conceptual legalization and to the transition from the idea of a spiritual communion arising out of the eucharist to the idea of a society, a hierarchical, institutional church society.

That is what it is, anyway, but the whole problem is to know which is the best concept to put first. Generally speaking I like to ask: by what concept do you arrive at the question? In the end the Church is certainly a society, but that is not what one should begin with. The first thing is the spiritual communion, a communion on the basis of the Word of God received in faith and grace, of which the sacraments are one of the principal vehicles. They are not the only ones, however: prayer is obviously a vehicle of grace, and so too is the pure, free action of God, who does what he wills. Thus the way into ecclesiology is not through society but through communion. This change in the application of the term 'mystical body' from the eucharist to the Church marks a transition to a more societal conception. And here I would take up a thesis put forward by the famous German canon lawyer Rudolph Sohm, who died, I think, in 1917. It is very controversial but nevertheless very exciting and opens up a great many questions. Sohm said that the *Decretum Gratiani* was in fact the first document of the Church-society, of the Church conceived of as a corporation, in other words conceived of socially (as a social corporation).

All Sohm's theses – or almost all of them – have been refuted, but the question remains, even if this is not actually the significance of the *Decretum Gratiani*, which one can also interpret as the last document of a sacramental Church. The question raised by Sohm is extremely important, and I once wrote a long article with a whole series of bibliographical notes, studying the thought of Sohm and refuting his positions in detail.

Moreover he often produced rather strange documentation, very disjointed and unsystematic, quoting a text from the fourth century alongside another from the twelfth, and so on.

Finally there is a moment, between Gregory VII – roughly around 1075 – and the middle of the twelfth century, i.e. about three-quarters of a century, when a change really takes place, though it is not a total one. For example, for the centenary of Thomas Aquinas in 1974 I wrote what I consider to be an important study on the basis of a text in the *Contra Gentiles* IV ch.76, in which Thomas Aquinas moves from the idea of people subject to a jurisdiction to the idea of the church by saying '*Iste populus est ecclesia*'. However, he distinguishes between the two concepts, the concept of the people which *qua* society has a jurisdiction, a power, and the concept of the Church which, for him, is defined only by faith and the sacraments of the faith (something more spiritual). It is true that *iste populus est ecclesia*, but it is very important to distinguish the two concepts and not to put all the stress on the idea of society.

On the question of the power of the papacy, do we not need to go back before Gregory VII? When would you put the beginnings of the claim to papal power conceived on the model of a society?

It's difficult to date exactly, but it goes back a very long way. On the purely ecclesial level the bishops of Rome expressed an awareness of their authority in the second century. This was considerably strengthened with Damasus, at the end of the fourth century, and the Popes of the fifth century. Moreover, the papacy indisputably inherited a legacy from imperial Rome. Rome was the capital and it has inherited an immense prestige: it is the city, *urbs*.

This idea has had varying influence, because there have been Popes like St Gregory the Great, for example, at the beginning of the seventh century (590-604), who conceived of his power in a much more spiritual way. And when the Archbishop of Constantinople claimed the title of universal bishop, Gregory replied to him that no one could lay claim to that title, which would suppress the authority of the others ('take the place of our brothers the bishops'). Now Gregory was also an organization man: he was a lawyer by training and, for example, he organized the temporal affairs of the Church of Rome very well. Then, in particular during the tenth century, 'the dark century of the Papacy', there were I don't know how many Popes who ultimately have left no interesting trace in the history of the Church (there were often family rivalries, assassinations and improbable stories).

However, the continuity is amazing. I am a great believer in the continuity of Rome, that of the Roman Church in the awareness that it has of itself. I was very impressed by the tomb of Cardinal Tardini, Secretary of State to Pius XII and John XXIII, which has on it as the only inscription *presbyter romanus* (priest of Rome). I think that that says a good deal for men like him or Cardinal Ottaviani; this Roman character is full of an ideology which has its greatness and which clearly weighs on us because of its claim to power. Vatican II tried to balance it to some degree by collegiality. Perhaps Vatican II was even rather short: I recall in Chapter III on the hierarchy that there was still the *cum et sub Petro* ('with or under Peter'). We asked the theological commission for rather less of it and Cardinal Ottaviani, who was president of the commission, replied that he had deleted *plures*, many; in fact he deleted two occurrences but added one...

I am convinced that the Bishop of Rome is in the succession of the *cathedra Petri*, the chair of Peter, and therefore of his authority, his teaching, his function in communion and the 'strengthening of the brethren' – which is what John-Paul II does constantly by his travels. But there is also the danger that there is too much Pope, too much central power. We also need to reflect a good deal on the actual notion of power; and we must remember the distinction between authority and power. For example, during the war, in 1942, General de Gaulle did not have any power in France, but he had authority. It is also necessary to distinguish between different kinds of power: spiritual power, disciplinary power, temporal power, and so on.

In the nineteenth century some people wanted to make a dogma of the idea that the Pope has a temporal power. That's incredible. We know very well how it came about in history: it was to resist the Lombards and their pressures and then, at the time of Gregory VII, to resist the emperor, who had all the south of Italy and all the north, with Germany etc. in the background, so that the Holy See was literally caught in a pincer movement. At this period it was impossible to think of independence without some territorial basis: it was land which gave autonomy, even to a spiritual power; hence this claim to temporal power. And that lasted, above all when the papacy was attracted by worldly rule. I have quoted a very good saying of John XXIII who remarked to an ambassador (I think it was the Canadian ambassador): 'We must brush off the imperial dust which has accumulated on the throne of St Peter.' John XXIII had intuitions like that; he did not work them out very far, but he felt them very strongly. What remains of that dust today? It's clear that there is some when one sees the Vatican with all the signs of earthly power. Clearly it's not just because the Swiss Guard have costumes designed by Michelangelo and carry halberds that they give an impression of power. Things are quite different at the World Council of Churches, where there are only offices and people in shirt sleeves, or at the Phanar in Istanbul – even if there one finds some décor and some dust of empire still clings to certain patriarchs or Orthodox bishops.

And what about the birth of scholastic and university theology?

That's certainly a real problem, one which meets up with the difficulties that we have with the Orthodox: the difference in rationalization in theology. Can one employ the concepts that we use for the things of nature in talking of God? I am convinced that from the Orthodox point of view this problem goes back a very long way: all the great theologians from the fourth century and the beginning of the fifth – John Chrysostom, the two Gregories, Basil – wrote a *Contra Eunomium*. Why? Because Eunomius claimed that he could know God and even define him

46

in philosophical terms. For the Orthodox, scholasticism is a kind of revival of Eunomius – I'm convinced that it is not that, but there is a real danger here.

Finally, the Church must always return to its heart. And one of the urgent priorities for us today is to form places of prayer, places of refreshment, a monastic spirit – the spirit, not necessarily the outward decorum and the temporal features. I experienced the Maredsous crisis: it largely arose from there; it was a real fortress.

Has Roman policy remained constant since Gregory VII? Does not Rome continue to want to reform the Church by the clergy rather than by a renewal of Christian communities (without, of course, opposing one to the other)? Recent books have drawn attention to the link between the crisis of faith and the crisis in the priesthood. What do you think about that?

It is certainly possible that Rome is still seeking reform through the clergy. That is understandable, in the sense that it has control over them: in them Rome has an organized army, obedient in principle, though I know hardly any other social body more independent than the clergy, freer in spirit and more original in the best sense of the word. Father Dujardin, Superior General of the Oratory, rightly remarks: 'In the past, every time the Church has been confronted with a crisis, it has coped with it by strengthening the body of the clergy through reforms.' In fact the Oratory of St Philip Neri is a good example, since it has been essentially a reassertion of the priesthood; however, we should note that it has also developed the teaching and training of lay people. And Fr Dujardin adds: 'Today the challenge of unbelief, or rather indifference, is such that it can only be met by all the people of God acting together. We have to take part in this effort at reviving the priestly conscience of Christian people.'

There have certainly been other reform projects in history. For example, in the thirteenth century Roger Bacon, a genius who was somewhat woolly-minded but original, had the idea of

47

reforming the Church by reforming studies. But the most interesting project was that of Jean Gerson, who wanted to reform the Church through the children.

Nowadays it seems that reform through the clergy is not enough, if that is still the plan of Rome, of the Curia – which I hesitate to say. In fact the Church is reforming itself in quite another way at present: it is reforming itself through the grass roots, and a great many priests are saying that they are learning from their faithful, lay people, and that without them they feel in a void. I myself feel this very clearly, deprived as I am at present of contacts with any kind of community. I understand this situation very well.

In a very interesting recent book entitled *Deux mille ans d'Église en question* (Two Millennia of the Church in Question), Fr Martelet is above all concerned to christologize the priesthood, to prevent the priest being defined too much by the community. That is a very noticeable trend at present, in which the community is theologized and indeed strengthened by the very important historical and theological foundations provided by people like my colleague Hervé Legrand. However, it would be stupid to contrast a 'christological tendency' with a 'pneumatological or community tendency' in any definition of the priest, since Christ will not do without the Church and the community will not do without the priest. Martelet is the first to recognize that, but he stresses a kind of vertical definition of the priest rather than a horizontal one. It is clear that you cannot set one against the other.

What do you think of Sunday assemblies without priests?

In a way they're magnificent. However, as I have already said, by the end of the century there will be no more priests in the whole of France than there are taxi drivers in Paris – 14,000. Now that is extremely serious, and I would gladly devote the rest of my life – little enough though there is of it – to that cause. It's very serious, since the Church cannot get on without priests. What is magnificent is that the laity are now setting to work.

48

The gospel and the Church continue, where the absence of the priest could have created a void, a kind of gulf into which what remains of Christianity could disappear. So I find that quite magnificent, and I encourage the laity to take initiatives in communities which have no priest as much as I can: to share the Word of God, to distribute the eucharist and so on. That's very good. I recall having quoted a remark made by Aragon about members of the Resistance who fell in their struggle, one which is engraved on the monument to the members of the Resistance of the Department of l'Ain near Oyonnax, where one of my fellow prisoners was shot. Aragon writes: 'Where I fall, my country is reborn.' I think that at present a number of the laity, without saying as much, are living out the truth that 'Where I am, the gospel continues; where I am, the gospel gains new life...'

Having said that, which I feel very deeply, I want nevertheless to note a very serious limit, to which in my view people do not pay enough attention. In particular, the bishops do not seem to me to be disturbed at what in fact is an extremely serious development: the danger of a certain Protestantizing of the conception that people have of the Church itself. In fact, in the last resort Sunday assemblies without priests are very close to what Protestant worship could be. This worship is undoubtedly very important, and I do not want to speak detrimentally of it in any way, to deny that it is a Christian assembly, communal praise of God, an expression and confession of the same faith together, and even, possibly, if the Protestant Lord's Supper is being celebrated, a memorial of the passion and the resurrection of Jesus – but the mass is different from that. And the Catholic Church is different from that. Moreover I am in no way doing down the Protestant pastor, for he would not want to be a priest. He would rightly reject what we include in the definition of the priest. So there is a very great danger for me. If we get used to this sort of thing, we shall come to lose sight of the fullness of Catholicism. And by Catholicism I do not mean the Roman system as such, but the continuity of the undivided Church, to which the Orthodox are even more qualified witnesses than

49

we are. From the Orthodox point of view it would be quite unthinkable that one could celebrate in the absence of a priest. Like us, they would certainly accept that it is better than nothing, but they themselves would bear extremely powerful witness in the opposite direction.

How do you see the present role of the Pope in the Church?

Let me talk first about the Pope in general, and then about John Paul II.

In talking about the Pope one has to begin with Peter. He is first of all one of the Twelve, but with two specific characteristics which are distinctive to him. On the one hand he receives by name, personally, in a particular way, that which the others will also receive, for example the status of apostle, of being 'a door' (in the Apocalypse, the apostles are the twelve doors), being a pastor (John 21), the power of the keys (which all receive in Matt.18 but which he receives first, in person, in Matt.16). On the other hand he often replies for the others, in place of the others; he speaks in the name of all: this is the element of 'representation' and 'personalization' of the whole apostolic college. We find that constantly in the Gospel, for example when Jesus asks, 'What do people say of the Son of Man?' Or when Jesus pays the temple tax for himself and for Peter, and in Acts, when Peter addresses the crowd first after Pentecost. That is important, even if it is history with a theological orientation. We can see how Peter is at the same time one of the Twelve, in their midst, and yet in a distinctive position.

It has to be accepted that the bishop of Rome is the successor of Peter – and also of Paul. It is not so easy to demonstrate this succession historically. But very soon there emerged in Rome the idea of a *cathedra Petri*, a chair of Peter, which represents the episcopal authority specific to Peter and which still exists in the Roman Church, albeit conjointly with the authority of Paul. In a large number of documents, for example canonizations, the Popes speak in the name of the apostles Peter and Paul. So I accept that the Pope is Peter's successor. He is in the college,

50

but in the college he occupies a particular position which allows him to speak, as did Peter in the midst of the Twelve, in a quite personal way, freely and independently. All the same, even in this instance he is bound up with the others, and without them he would not be anything at all: bound to the Church by faith, he is also dependent on the faith of the Church. That is why, moreover, he is never completely alone. And I recall very well that in the famous *nota praevia explicativa* – the explanation preceding the *modi* added to Chapter III of *Lumen Gentium* which caused difficulties for a minority at the Council – the Pope is not said to act *solus* but *seorsim*. Not in solitude, but in a personal way.

That is where the question of the power that he uses arises. Is this strictly personal power, or is it the power of the college exercised by the one who is its head? I have not yet completely made up my mind on this question, but I think nevertheless that I shall keep to the view put forward by Karl Rahner: the power is always the power of the college. In effect, Rahner says, there cannot be two supreme powers. Now it is certain that by divine right the College of Bishops enjoys supreme power in the Church, as does the Council. Clearly the College and the Council also include the Pope, which is why there is also an alternative theory according to which these are two different powers, but not sufficiently distinct. The one always implies the other; i.e. the power of the college always implies that of the Pope. Here there is a risk of moving towards a monarchical idea. This idea was put forward in the Middle Ages and at the Renaissance. Ulrich Horst's book shows how, at the beginning of the sixteenth century, in the preparations for the Fifth Lateran Council (1512-1517, this theory of the papal monarchy was supported by a large number of theologians, including Dominicans (Cajetan, for example, upheld it with arguments which in my view were sheer dialectical stratagems).

The monarchical theory, according to which everything depends on one (*monos*) who communicates his power to all the bishops, was still held at Vatican II, in particular by Fr Gagnebet and many others. But this theory cannot be sustained. It is *historically* indefensible. For eight or ten centuries the Popes never intervened in the creation of bishops or the nomination of bishops. For example, a study has been made of the 620 or 640 English bishops from the evangelization of England until the beginning of the twelfth century: in no case did the Pope intervene, either for particular individuals or to create a bishopric. Similarly, at one point St Augustine divided his see, which he thought to be too large, without asking anyone. So the monarchical theory in the strict sense of the word – everything depending on the Pope as its source, as its cause – seems to me quite untenable.

However, something of the monarchical idea remains if this consists in accepting that there is an authority which settles debates, a kind of authority for arbitration. But that is not monarchical in the strict sense of the word. It is the exercise of a power peculiar to the Bishop of Rome as successor to Peter within the college.

It is difficult to be more precise. I recall that when I wrote in these terms on another occasion, Abbé Journet, who went on to become a cardinal, criticized me. But he never really understood collegiality, nor the famous trilogy of priest-king-prophet, which had very great consequences when he spoke of laity and priests. For him the trilogy was uniquely hierarchical – priest, king, saviour – whereas one can apply the trilogy of priest-king-prophet to lay people, as the Council did (cf. Chapter IV of *Lumen Gentium* on the laity).

To go back to distinctively papal power, can one be more precise about how it is exercised?

Paul VI indicated this particular power very clearly at least twice at the Council. First, on the very day that the second period was inaugurated, he presented a *motu proprio* creating the synod of bishops even before the Council had decided on this itself in *Christus Dominus*, the decree on the ministry of bishops: he wanted in this way to mark his independence from the Council. The second example (though there would certainly be others) was when the Council had already voted on the text on ecumenism. Paul VI introduced nineteen *modi* which did not really change the text but in some cases introduced important nuances.

What about John-Paul II?

First I would like to talk about his personality. I knew Mgr Woytyla at the Council, though his contributions at that time – which were noted by Fr de Lubac in his book on Vatican II as 'quite remarkable and widely noted' – never made much of an impression on me. But I got to know him above all when work was being done on schema XIII (*Gaudium et Spes*) and I even collaborated with him directly. I remember the impression that he made on me – and I even noted it immediately in my diary. As the young Archbishop of Cracow (he was not yet a cardinal) he made a truly prophetic impression on me: he had a kind of charisma, an air which was quite irresistible (I think that those are the very words that I used in my diary). This extraordinary charisma is obvious. But there is more to him than that. In all the vast number of his texts and speeches – there are perhaps too many of them; they are so numerous that one cannot follow them all – he always goes to the root of things. If you take all the speeches that he gave in and around Lyons when he was in France in autumn 1986 you have a complete and very invigorating catechesis.

So this man seems to me to be a grace given to Christians and to our age: coming from the East, a Slav, he has a new contribution to make to the Church. Of course you can criticize him, for example in connection with his travels which have 'too much of the Pope' about them and do not allow him really to listen and to take note of what is going on in the local churches. Nevertheless, I believe that he sees a good deal, since he is a very perceptive man with a great sensitivity to people and cultures. These journeys also restore confidence to the local churches, where that is necessary. And in that respect he exercises his role of strengthening the brethren, as he himself says constantly.

He also always introduces himself as 'Bishop of Rome and universal pastor'. Clearly, this title 'universal pastor' pushes the truth right to the limit, but one can understand it and accept it. It may be that not everything in his thought and his theology is perfect. It has often been said that on several points his thought is somewhat Tridentine, but the Council itself has traces of Tridentinism: Alberigo showed it recently, even if some of his quotations are debatable. Vatican II sought to remain within the lines of the tradition, but it put Trent and Vatican I in a new context. For example, the papacy is set over against the new background of collegiality; it is what I call a re-reception.

On the other hand it is possible that the Holy Father, while coming from the East, is not totally informed about the Orthodox tradition. He talks of it often, and even well. I can only agree when I often see him taking up a phrase of which I am very fond: 'The Church must breathe through both lungs' – provided that he does not identify the Orthodox Church with the Eastern Church and the Catholic Church with the Western Church. So he attaches great importance to the Orthodox tradition. But is he aware of its depths? Perhaps less than John XXIII, who had lived in the East, in Bulgaria and in Constantinople, and who had the kind of basic instinct which allowed him to grasp the depths of the reality of the Orthodox Church. Perhaps John Paul II does not have this charism to the same degree, but beyond question ecumenism remains one of the priorities of his mission as Bishop of Rome and universal pastor. From an ecumenical point of view, he has said a good deal and done a good deal. If this has not always been successful, it is because there are other aspects: his Marian theology and his position on particular ethical problems, which remain a difficulty for our Protestant brothers.

You have already expressed your feelings about the importance of episcopal conferences in the government of the Church, but could you say something more about how you see relations between the bishops and the Pope?

The Orthodox stress this point: the papacy is not the result of a sacrament, and therefore the primacy of the Pope over the bishops is canonical and juridical, not sacramental. What the ordained ministers and the bishop are to the local church, the Pope is to the universal Church. Now under Pius XII there was a tendency to make the Pope the deputy head – the concept already appears in St Thomas and throughout scholasticism – of the mystical body, including the order of grace. That is certainly debatable.

It is a fact that one often goes to Rome. It is a fact that when John-Paul II travels – and he went on about thirty visits in 1986 – he attracts millions of people. Sometimes more than a million people gather in front of him. And quite apart from the fact that he is a media star, there is something else: the desire to see the Pope, the desire to see someone who is as it were the icon of unity, the icon of communion. And that is very important. The Pope truly has that position in the Catholic Church. This extraordinary symbolic value cannot be created artificially. If one were to say: let's elect someone who is going to be the representative of a whole continent or even of the whole world, things would not go on as they do.

I recently read in *Irénikon* a whole section on the preparation for the great and holy council that the Orthodox have now been working on for a very long time (and for the Orthodox the preparation is already a conciliar reality which, moreover, involves all the representatives of the Churches, even if no actual decisions are taken). The Orthodox do not have this personalized icon of unity. Their unity is synodical. And that is no small thing.

So it is necessary to take account of two logics of unity: a logic of primacy and a synodical logic. The first predominated in the West, extended to the Americas, and then throughout the world. The Roman Catholic Church or, if you prefer, the patriarchy of the West ended up by concentrating unity on one man, with the powers relating to this role: if there is a charisma, there are also the means for fulfilling this role, a certain authority, though at the risk of ending up in too monarchical a logic.

The Eastern Church, which has also spread throughout the world today – with emigrations, persecutions, missions and diaspora – has a synodical logic which puts the emphasis on exchanges between local churches.

These two logics are authentic and not contradictory: a fully Catholic Church – if we achieve unity one day – must implement both logics, that of the primacy and that of the synod.

A last point to be noted in passing: the notion of the patriarchy of the West is important: the purely Latin Councils are not ecumenical councils but councils of the patriarchy of the West.

You have spoken of priests, bishops and the Pope, but there is an ordained ministry which remains separate, that of deacons. What do you think of that?

I was one of those behind the restoration of the diaconate, and a supporter of the possibility of the diaconate being conferred on married men. At that time I had links with Fr Kramer, the German who was and has continued to be the moving force behind this movement. Then, during the Council, during the fourth period, in Rome, under the presidency of Cardinal Doepfner and Cardinal Silva Enriquez, we had a meeting at which I gave a lecture. It was published later, but I am no longer happy with it.

I think and I acted in the following way. The diaconate is an ordained ministry. It is a 'degree' of the sacrament of orders, which includes diaconate, presbyterate and episcopate. (I do not like this term degree very much because in fact the diaconate is not necessarily an order which precedes the presbyterate and is dependent on it; rather, it is parallel to the presbyterate and, like it, depends on the bishop.) There are several aspects to be noted if one is to understand the significance of the diaconate.

1. The diaconate does away with the monopoly of the priest as minister, since for a long time the presbyterate was considered the one and only ministry. To introduce the ordained deacon, i.e. someone who has received the sacrament of orders, was to

abolish this kind of monopoly and leave room for other ministries which I shall be mentioning later.

2. It is quite a new development. Moreover, the Church of France has been rather slow to introduce the diaconate. Several bishops were reluctant, several were opposed to it because they thought that it could harm Catholic Action. Since then 300 deacons have been ordained in France, but there are many more in Germany, in Chile, and above all in the United States, where they really are very numerous. However, the most interesting thing is to see the effects of this new development in other areas and on the idea of ministry. In particular, the reflections and regular meetings that have been prompted by the introduction of the permanent diaconate have allowed the question of the call (or vocation) to the diaconate to be renewed: this is not primarily a subjective question, a personal desire, but the call of a community which needs a deacon (or a priest).

3. There really are personal vocations. There are men who are ready to accept this ministry if they are called to it and who do not seek to become priests. The ministry shows the notion of service which was one of the great values of the Council. I brought that out before the Council in an article which I had published in the collected volume *L'Episcopat et L'Église universelle* (The Episcopate and the Universal Church). It appeared in 1962 and many bishops read it; at least, many of the French-speaking ones.

I remember how when Karl Barth came to Rome – twice – *Ad limina apostolorum* (to quote the title of his book about it), theologians were chosen as his conversation partners according to the various schemata that they had worked on very closely. I was nominated to reply to questions about the schema on liturgy, and one of the questions which Barth asked me was, 'What in your view is the essential idea of the Council?' I replied, 'Service.' I think that this idea played a very major role in the Council and that it has continued to inspire the ministries of priests, bishops and particularly deacons, since the deacon is defined as being the servant: he is ordained *non ad presbyterium sed ad ministrandum*. And that is very happy. That is what would seem to me to be an essential part of the restoration of the diaconate, which in fact principally has married men in view.

One question remains open: that of the diaconate for women. Deaconesses did exist. They were ordained at Byzantium and at Antioch – the two places where they were most active – with precisely the same words as the deacons, and at the same place – in front of the altar. The women of today have much more of a place in the Church than the deaconesses ever had; these deaconesses virtually disappeared from the twelfth century on in the East and never really existed in the West. If the diaconate were restored for women, that would be a new creation. Be this as it may, bishops – like the German bishops – have specifically called for a restoration of the diaconate for women, not only in a personal report to the Holy See (I know about this because I worked on it) but in their federal synod. Such a development would be very important, for if the diaconate is the first degree of orders that would be a very interesting opening, though I personally subscribe to the Roman document against the ordination of women to the presbyterate and the episcopate.

– 5 –

Faith, Spiritual Life and Theology

Theology must always return to the source of its inspiration: God himself. People today feel the need for a new approach. Certainly it is easier and almost truer to pray than to speak of God properly, but how do you see this question in the light of your personal experience?

That's very true: it is easier to pray than to talk about God. First of all, this word God does not really have a content of itself. We give it one: the Creator, the Lord, the Ruler, the end of all things, but in itself the word does not have any content. If one wants to give a content to God over and above this sovereignty, great though that is (see Islam and Judaism), one must say: God is Father, Son and Holy Spirit. That is the trinitarian vision. It was very active at Vatican II, and it was relatively new. I'm afraid that the vision of God at Vatican I was monotheistic (this point has been outlined by Pinto de Oliveira), without developing this trinitarian mystery. Things were different at Vatican II, from the first chapters in *Lumen Gentium* and *Ad Gentes*: the church is an earthly and historical revelation, but by the communication of the grace of the trinitarian mystery.

While recognizing the practicality of the custom, I regret that at mass the celebrant intones the creed by saying 'I believe in one God' and then the assembly joins in with 'the Father almighty', and so on. That might encourage the wrong idea that there is a divine essence within which one should *then* distinguish three aspects or persons. Even we theologians are led to think of the Father, the Son and the Spirit as following one another in that order, whereas they are absolutely simultaneous, perfectly co-existing. The Orthodox are right to say that in God everything is trinitarian. I would not go so far as to say God is God *because* he is Father, but he is certainly God by being Father, and not according to something anterior to this quality. I am equally aware of the charge sometimes laid against us by the Orthodox that first we presuppose a Father-Son dyad and then their relationship of love, the Spirit. But on the other hand I think that they are unjust to St Augustine. It is only after having commented on scripture in connection with the mystery of the Trinity that Augustine suggests the analogy of the human spirit. After all, we are in the image of God! It is not a matter of thinking of an essence and then going on to discern faculties.

I would like to add a few words on what is sometimes called apophatic or negative theology. It is not really negative, but an expression of the positive in an apparently negative form, as at the Council of Chalcedon. In reality the knowledge that one can have of God, the expressions that one can use for him, are already far beyond reality. I think that it was Gregory of Nazianzus, or perhaps Master Eckhart, who said, 'You who have the names and have none of them, you are all the beings and you are none of them, you are beyond everything', and we ourselves say in the Preface, 'light beyond all light'. In fact we have to see that no matter what we attribute to God, we never know the divine mode under which that exists. For example, the justice of God is identical with his mercy. Or we speak of God almighty and tend to imagine that divine power is human power to the supreme degree. But it is not that. It is far beyond that. The divine manner of being omnipotent escapes us completely. Father Varillon, whom I knew well and loved, once wrote a book on the humility of God and another on the suffering in God. These are fine and profound books, and I only regret that he treated his subjects in too literary a fashion. For one can only speak of the humility of God in a very humble way, not with such an abundance and wealth of style and imagery. Finally, in theology, I am very fond of the doxologies, of which there are a great many in St Paul and in the present Breviary. For the doxologies, i.e.

the praises of God, express the divine mystery, but in a kind of poetic form, full of images, which I believe to be ultimately richer than more conceptual, more abstract expressions.

For me personally, faith in God comes from my childhood; I have never really doubted it, though it would not be true that I have never had doubts. However, my faith has remained what it has been from the beginning, namely a very paternal idea, God the Father. Moreover we know that when God is spoken of in the New Testament, with very few exceptions, it is the Father who is referred to (as Karl Rahner has shown). I began with this notion of God. And my personal devotion is still along those lines, all the more so since it is very much orientated on the psalms.

But there is no doubt that subsequently I had a more active perception of Jesus Christ, in the novitiate and as a student, partly thanks to my colleagues, and in particular thanks to Fr Maydieu. Then, by reflection, I came to the Holy Spirit. When I began working on my three volumes on the Holy Spirit – *I Believe in the Holy Spirit* – first of all I made a brief survey of my past publications and saw that I had written and published eighteen or nineteen articles on the Spirit. So I had been preoccupied with the Spirit for quite a long time, but there were always other specific commitments and deadlines which I had to meet.

My view of God has always been biblical. God is the living God, the one to whom one can say 'My God'. Not, however, in an individualistic sense, for the 'I' of the psalms is not that of an isolated individual; the 'I' represents the people of God, and each individual represents the people of God in a particular way. God is the living God who has a plan for the world. I am convinced that our ways are guided, in other words that we have to discern a call, an occasion.

I often also think of eternal life. I think that one has it now. That is spelt out in St John, but I think of it in an existential, real way. Like everyone else, I know that this eternal life now must emerge, after death, in some kind of exaltation towards God, in whose presence it will be completely revealed. But one

61

cannot imagine it, any more than one can imagine how a chrysalis will become a butterfly, or cherry blossom, so beautiful in April, will become fruit. I often think about it, but each time I end up with a mystery which I cannot see clearly.

You have always attached great importance to the figure of Mary in achieving a balance between faith and theology. What would you say about that today?

I'm glad to talk about the Virgin Mary. When I reflect, I can see three different periods in my life.

The first period, my childhood and the beginning of my religious life, is the one in which I had a quite childlike Marian devotion, very simple, as towards a mother watching over me. I remember that sometimes I put the word 'Ave' at the top of some of my papers and on my copy of the *Summa*, in so doing imitating St Thomas. (In the Vatican we have the autograph of the greater part of the *Contra Gentiles*, and St Thomas writes 'Ave' in the margin several times.)

When I began to do theology in a more active way, a second period began; it corresponds almost exactly with the pontificate of Pius XII. At that time there was quite a frenetic development of Mariology. I have even used the expression 'galloping Mariology', rather as people used to speak of galloping consumption, an illness which spread in an abnormal and ultra-rapid fashion. The Pope himself prepared the dogmatic definition of the bodily assumption of Mary Mother of God – I was not at all in favour of that, since historically the ancient evidence is very sparse and we can no longer accept that the present faith of the church has a revelatory value, even if one can draw certain consequences from divine motherhood. At the Council I witnessed the sequel to this galloping Mariology, since in the preparatory commission – which was no longer that of the Council itself, thank God – Fr Balič, who was from the Holy Office, very powerful at Rome and very dynamic – had had as many Mariologists nominated as he could, for example the President of the Mariological Conference of Canada and the Secretary of the Spanish Mariologists. For France he had nominated a member of the commission for which I was just a consultant, Mgr Dubois, Archbishop of Besançon, theologically a complete nonentity – he did not get a single vote when there were elections to nominate the members of the Council commissions – but a Mariologist to the tips of his fingers, in my view excessively so. Laurentin was among the consultants, but he did not in fact do what Balič expected of him: I recall a day when I was sitting in front of them and Balič said to him, 'You've betrayed us.' Balič wanted the Council to proclaim Mary mediatrix of all the graces, queen, corredemptrix.

During the Council I followed the laborious composition of ch. VIII of *Lumen Gentium* very closely. That was a great moment because up to that point in the Catholic Church there had been a kind of movement which isolated mediations and magnified them to excess. The pope was isolated from the college, but the Council put him back in the college, as head, yet in its midst; the religious were isolated from the life of other Christians, but the Council gave them back their place in the universal quest for sanctity; the priest was isolated from the faithful, but one can now see how much they have come together. And Mary was isolated from all the saints, from the church itself: she was made a kind of intermediary – to use a saying of St Bernard which I myself don't much like: 'Mary is the neck which joins the head to the body!' No, Mary is in the body. I much prefer St Augustine's saying: '*Membrum, membrum ecclesiae, excellentissimum membrum, sed membrum ecclesiae*' (a member, a member of the church, an eminent member, but a member of the church). Now just as the Council restored the Pope to the college, so Mary was restored to the mystery of Christ and the Church. That's very healthy. I am completely in agreement with ch. VIII of *Lumen Gentium*: Mary has a very considerable place in the mystery of Christ and the Church. I have often told my Protestant friends at meetings of the ecumenical movement that they will have to come to Mary one day. That is what is already happening with some of them; not just at Taizé, which is very advanced from this point of view, but even among a number of pastors and theologians, though they are still isolated.

63

From this point of view Calvin has an inadequate christological position. It is not wrong, though. Calvin certainly accepts Chalcedon. However, he is happier with Mary Mother of Christ than Mary Mother of God, as the Council of Ephesus put it. By contrast Luther attached great importance to the Council of Ephesus, regarding it as the main council: in affirming that Mary is Mother of God, Ephesus affirmed that Christ is truly God in such a way that is it is impossible to separate humanity and divinity, even in filiation. Calvin speaks in a somewhat Nestorian way, although he is not Nestorian: Mary is the mother of Christ. Mary is much more than the purely biological mother of a child, Jesus, who moreover was to be Son of God. Mary is truly the mother of the Firstborn. That is how I see my third period. The second period was a period of struggle against galloping Mariology; I wrote several articles and reviews, I had a small book published entitled *Le Christ, Marie et l'Église*, which was part of this struggle. Now I see myself in the mainstream of Catholic doctrine, and moreover, Fr Balič himself has taken account of it, particularly in the Mariological Congresses, for example by inviting Protestants, Orthodox and Anglicans. During the Council itself there were nevertheless considerable discussions. I was well informed about them by Mgr Philips: though he was as much a Mariologist as all the Louvain people, including Cardinal Suenens, he kept a balanced view. He had discussions with Balič, who brought him a new schema every day, in Latin, since he had an amazing capacity for work, and they would go over it at lunch time. They both knew that the Pope did not want the 'corredemptrix', and each knew that the other knew it, but they never said as much. And one day at the Holy Office, the place where the famous Wednesday meetings were held, I took part in a small meeting which was to discuss the question of Mary corredemptrix – which was eliminated – and mediatrix of all the graces, which I criticized, in particular in connection with the sacramental graces. The Council took up the expression 'mediatrix' again, but explained it appropriately.

An Orthodox brother said to me: 'Mary is the Church.' And I am fond of talking with my Orthodox brothers, because they always bring us down to essentials. Yes, but Mary is not all the Church. Fr Louis Bouyer speaks of an 'eschatological icon of the Church'. Mary is the realization of the *res*, but the Church is also a *sacramentum*. Now I believe that it is important when talking of the Church as sacrament also to see that it is the reality of salvation and not just a sign and instrument. In this church Mary represents the *res*, the perfect fruit obtained, and does not represent the *sacramentum*. The well-known formula of Cardinal Journet is correct: Mary has sanctified greatness but she does not have hierarchical greatness. I wrote elsewhere that Mary was one of the faithful in the church, a lay person. I won't go over that again today, but Mary must have her place in the Church.

Thirty-four years after the publication of your 1953 book Towards a Theology of the Laity, *could you take stock of the situation, which is still very much an ongoing one?*

The deliberately modest title of this book meant that in it I only wanted to offer material for further research. It was summed up in a review in the bulletin of the Mission de France as saying: 'The spiritual for the clergy, the temporal for the laity.' That is certainly not my position in this work. From a theological perspective I was talking about the participation of the laity in the three offices of Christ, because this schema – it must not be absolutized, but the Council took it up – makes it possible to give a proper indication of the various aspects of the role of the laity: in sacerdotal activity (priest), in witness and the proclamation of faith (prophet), and in the organization of an earthly destiny (king). Beyond question we are much further on today than in 1953. There is no longer any need to define the laity in relation to the clergy which, I grant, is rather what I did, though I gave the laity a major place: that was my aim and that was the result. However, Fr Daniélou, who had very keen insights and fell on sensitive points like a hawk on a fieldmouse, noted in *Dieu vivant* that I had defined the laity in terms of the clergy. Today it is the case, rather, that the clergy need to be defined in relation to the laity, who are quite simply members

65

of the people of God animated by the Spirit. One of the results both of the Council and of the secularization of the social sphere has been a major new emphasis on baptism. The laity are primarily the baptized. Christians – clergy and lay – are a people of those who have been baptized.

Since then there have been all the contemporary developments in the life of the church. In France, especially with the lack of priests, the increase in the average age of the clergy and the shrinkage in the fabric of the rural church, lay people are taking over the great tasks of the church so that it can go on existing. This is a very important phenomenon, above all in France. In Latin America, with its basic communities, things are rather different. In Poland, where the clergy are still numerous, things are different again.

The laity therefore often take initiatives which are very much in the spirit of the gospel. I have often said, and I must say it again, that we are in one of the most evangelistic centuries of all history. I know that it is a century of unbelief and religious indifference, that it is also the century of the expansion of Islam, but among the minority of faithful who truly believe, it is a really evangelistic century. I am amazed to see the commitment of a large number of faithful who are concerned with drug-addicts and delinquents, but also with immigrants, illiterates, catechetical work, etc, so that there can be a church.

All that benefits a great deal from the development of the idea of charisms in the sense of individual gifts for the benefit of all. The Council after Pius XII with his 1943 encyclical *Mystici Corporis* – which went with his very institutional ecclesiology – put a stress on charisms (*Lumen Gentium*, Chapter II, 12). Since then, there has been the whole of the 'charismatic' movement in another direction, and that is why I prefer to call it more simply 'the renewal', which is playing a very major role today. This renewal needs to be warned about certain internal dangers – and it is usually quite clear-sighted – but it is also aware of the spiritual gifts which must benefit the community.

The question arises of knowing in what conditions gifts are simply services and when they merit the name of ministries. I made a contribution to the Assembly of Bishops in Lourdes in 1973 and said that I would recognize the existence of 'ministries' if three conditions were realized simultaneously:

1. There must be an essential service for the Church: sweeping a room is a service, but it is neither essential nor peculiar to the Church; on the other hand catechesis, celebration and diaconia are essentials.

2. It has to be stable, in such a way that one can count on it, and not something occasional, a service done in passing.

3. It should be recognized at the highest level, if possible by the bishop. The bishop often sanctions a 'canonical mission', whether this term is used or not. But it can also be recognized by a parochial announcement: for example, Mr or Mrs X are responsible for chaplaincy work at a particular college.

In these conditions I think that one can talk of ministry. I am very well aware that 'service' and 'ministry' are two translations of the same Greek word, *diakonia*. But these two different terms go back to diffent contexts: the word 'ministry' says much more than 'service', since it expresses an assured function in the service of the Church, in accordance with the conditions that I have just indicated.

It is true that despite all this there is still a good deal of clericalism in the Church. Every week I get evidence of clergy who retain a taste for authority. In the old days they did a bit of everything – they were a kind of one-man band – and many still want to control everything and even have a hand in everything. And yet, God knows that I would not want to criticize lightly priests who often have to live in difficult conditions.

Today people no longer want to be objects but subjects. And this concern could be bound up with the modern democratic feeling, although one cannot properly talk of democracy in the Church. People want to be free and responsible subjects. That is true in all spheres: in political life, in the Church generally and more specifically in the local churches as over against the central Roman authority. At the last synod we saw bishops asking that the local churches should be allowed to live their own lives and make decisions at their level. In itself that is quite

67

healthy and quite proper. The laity need to be subjects. That is true of women in particular, and many of them are leaving the churches today because they are disappointed at the inadequate role that is being assigned to them. There is still much to be said on this matter. I hold to the first view expressed in the issue of *Concilium* on *Invisible Women in the Church and in Theology* (210), although because of its excesses this issue brings out what one might call the 'infantile malady of feminism'. However, it contains much that is true and profound. That is one of the reasons for the present crisis in any case: there are people who do not feel themselves sufficiently to be subjects: women, young people, all those who feel somewhat discriminated against.

The year 1987 is also that of the celebration of the twelfth centenary of Nicaea II, which legitimized the cult of icons. In the wider sphere of cultural and cultic representations, are there not those who say that in the period which has followed Vatican II there has been a kind of iconoclasm?

This is an immense problem with a great many aspects. I can only take up one, beginning from the contrast between faith and religion which was advocated above all by Barth and taken up in France by Fr Liégé, and from what is called 'popular religion'. Popular religion can be roughly described as an attachment to certain practices as a result of family or local tradition, practices relating to the baptism of small children, first communion, with its so-called 'traditional' practices (which largely go back to the seventeenth century), marriage and so on. The question has been raised by numerous colleagues in the Church and in the universities. It is quite clear that above all since Vatican II there has been considerable pruning back of these traditional forms to which many people had remained or still remain attached. There was an article in the *Figaro Magazine* of 23 November 1985 which, though wrong in its main thrust and on many points of detail, used an interesting expression in connection with this kind of pruning that I have mentioned. It spoke of a deforestation which ended up by making land vulnerable to erosion. There is a true insight here. Unfortunately this theme of reaction against deforestation and erosion has often been taken up in an aggressive way. That's a pity, since the problem is real and quite profound, though it is difficult to identify. I am convinced on the one hand that faith, in the sense in which Fr Liégé speaks of it, needs to be reclothed: faith must be clothed; it needs a cultural expression, ceremonies, art, beauty, literature, music. However, our present cultural milieu does not lend itself to that, even if there is a real spiritual sense among certain artists, above all outside the Church. What there used to be of a cultural expression of Catholicism and Christianity in these various spheres of art, literature and music is quite weak today, or is limited to what are often marginal groups, in a kind of sub-culture.

However, I would add that in this sphere, as in many others, there are temporary replacements and transfers. This is a category which I find useful in many spheres; there are many things which hae been changed without being suppressed – they are simply done differently. Here there are kinds of transfers, temporary replacements of the old culture. For example there is the taste for icons which is quite widespread today. There are very lively popular places like La Chapelle of the Miraculous Medal in the rue du Bac; and pilgrimages, for example the pilgrimage of the Rosary, which is truly becoming a place of evangelization and which adds a dimension of evangelization and spiritual training to the type of popular religion characteristic of the great pilgrimages. In music there is the whole work of Fr Gouzes: he has rediscovered a sacral dimension, in part inspired by the Eastern tradition which is still alive among the Orthodox. There is sometimes a danger of élitism or aestheticism there (neo-Byzantine, Eastern, sentimental) but these new developments are important when so many values are breaking apart.

Do we also have to reproach ourselves today for the pruning back that I have mentioned – or iconoclasm, if one wants to use that word, the collapse of popular religious practice which started well before Vatican II? The fact remains that in many areas there is from 1 to 3% practice, and that is quite new. In the parish where I come from, one with more than 1,500

69

inhabitants, there is only one person at high mass. So there are considerable problems.

Among the values which some people say have been 'eroded', there is a theological tradition which is dear to you, Thomism. How has your thinking developed in this connection?

I'll gladly tell you about that. But first of all, I would like to say how I was introduced to St Thomas. Abbé Daniel Lallement, who later became a professor at the Catholic Institute, was sub-deacon in my home town of Sedan. It was during the First World War. He held meetings for boys who were more or less destined for the seminary. I was not part of the group originally, but I joined later and visited this Abbé often. With him we read St Thomas along with Cajetan, always inseparably, and I was introduced to both of them equally. Being young, I admired them but could not always follow what they said. However, as soon as I could, with the little money I had, I bought a Leonine edition, so that I had the text with Cajetan. Then, when I was seventeen, I went to the Carmelite seminary in Paris, and there Abbé Lallement introduced me to Thomism, beginning with the life of St Thomas. I liked that very much. As one who has always had a taste for history and already had it at that time, I approached the thought of St Thomas through history and not just through Cajetan. At the 'Catho', the Catholic Institute, I had Thomistic professors – Lallement, Maritain, Fr Blanche OP and so on.

What do I owe to St Thomas, that I have gone back to him so often? First of all a certain spiritual structure. That's what makes him relevant even today. His ideas are well-ordered.

Then there is a sense of openness and even dialogue. Because St Thomas, with his incredible dialectical power, spent all his life looking for new texts, making new translations for himself, discussing with all the people of his age: Jews, Moslems, Averroists, Augustinians and so on. Thomism is a matter of being open to dialogue. There is a real spiritual structure that I owe to St Thomas and for which I am infinitely grateful to him.

70

However, beyond question I developed, and in a way even parted company with Thomism: I will say how and on what points.

I came to develop above all through history and ecumenism, because I have done a good deal of history without being a professional historian, and I have practised ecumenism. That gave me a good deal of work and made me see the Thomistic structure as a system from another perspective. I am even very fond of Péguy's saying, 'Not the true, but the real,' provided that it is properly understood. I have devoted my life to the truth; I often think that it is really the woman in my life. Indeed I have often written *Veritas domina mea* at the head of my texts. And I have often quoted the saying of Madame Swetchine, 'I have loved truth as one loves a person.' I hold to the truth, but the real, i.e. truth with historicity, with its concrete state in becoming, in time, is something else. That is very important, for the Thomism which some have held, or perhaps still hold, is basically a philosophy of identity in continuity with Parmenides. Whereas St Thomas, with his thesis of 'power' and 'action', has a dynamic conception of being. Fr Sertillanges remarked that in Thomism, being is 'dynamogenic'. Moreover, from the beginning, in commenting on Boethius' *De Trinitate*, Thomas distinguishes the *id quod est* and the *id quo est* – if you like, this is a distinction between essence and existence. But what is interesting is the *id quod est*, what really exists. Now what exists is historical.

Moreover, there is a danger in Thomism, although I do not think that Thomas himself succumbed to it – I shall say why in a moment – a danger of homogeneity almost at any price, to the degree that the human beings are themselves conceived of in the manner of natural things. I think that this is quite a widespread danger in Catholic metaphysical reflection, and that one will already find it in St Anselm and in Thomas himself, at least as a risk to which they did not actually succumb. Thomas in fact says quite clearly (*Contra Gentiles* IV.11): 'The person is the highest form of being', of the '*id quod est*'. That is basically a very modern idea, and J.B.Metz wrote his thesis on this subject,

71

thinking that Thomism is anthropocentrism. There is a profound insight which needs to be followed up and developed here. I am not sure whether Thomas developed it himself. I personally would prefer to keep to certain Orthodox thinkers like Vladimir Lossky, whom I knew well and admired: he distinguished between nature and person. These thinkers derive their reflection from that of the Fathers of the Church – the great Cappadocians of the fourth and fifth centuries - on the Trinity. I think that that goes a long way, and that there is an ontology of the person which cannot be reduced to a pure ontology of nature. The ontology of the person is much more relational and historical. So we leave what could be the heritage of Parmenides to follow a biblical thread. In the Bible, when God gives his name, it is not 'I am he who is' (*to on*), as the Septuagint translates it and as Gilson has taken it up in what he calls the 'metaphysics of the Exodus', but something much more: 'I am he who is there' (*Dasein*, but not as Heidegger understands it): 'I am there with you', 'I will be' – for the verb is future: 'I will be who I will be', 'I will be there with you'. So this is a historicity of God.

I would very much endorse a remark by my colleague, teacher and friend, Fr Chenu, who said that 'our time is a dimension of the eternity of God'. Clearly this formula calls for an explanation, but it is true that by the incarnation God has become the subject of a history. A human history has entered into the eternity of God.

So that is why, even now, I am much indebted to St Thomas. When I still had my study, I often went back to the *Summa* and sometimes to the commentaries: I spent a long time with the biblical commentaries of St Thomas on St John and St Paul and, of course, the *Quaestiones Disputatae*, where he explains himself more.

However, I have gone somewhat beyond the Thomism I was taught to begin with.

What has been the role of Le Saulchoir in the development of your relationship to St Thomas?

When I was at the Catholic Institute between 1921 and 1924 – they were three very happy and fervent years in an atmosphere which was both traditional and very free – I still had close links with Abbé Lallement, who was a man who made a strong impression on those who came under his direction. I also had links with Jacques Maritain: every month I went to Meudon, and each year I followed the retreat preached – first at Versailles and then at Meudon – by Fr Garrigou-Lagrange.

Basically I have dissociated myself a good deal from Maritain the philosopher. I recognize the greatness of Maritain in his intellectual charity and the depth of his spiritual life; Raïssa's book *Les Grandes Amitiés*, with its very fine title, 'The Great Friendships', is very significant in this respect. I recognize Maritain's considerable contribution to morality, ethics and the political philosophy of democracy. There is much fine and great Maritain. But there was also this kind of Thomistic ontology, which in fact depended on Jean de Saint-Thomas. For that is what he was doing at Meudon: he would read us a page of Jean de Saint-Thomas, often very subtle, on points which he himself qualified with 'adamantine' distinctions, and he developed all this with such fervour and such seduction that we 'drank in' his words.

I dissociated myself from this approach. And it is a fact that Jacques Maritain did not have much sympathy with Le Saulchoir, where I went next. There were deep-seated reasons for that: Le Saulchoir was the historical approach to St Thomas, not in order to relativize that which cannot be relativized but in order to put his thought in a period, since everything is historical – absolutely everything, including the Bible and Jesus. That is what made two different groups. And I myself, first by instinct and then thanks to the teaching and friendship of my elders – Chenu in particular and also Féret – went in this direction, which I pursued in ecumenism and the rest.

So you parted company with 'neo-Thomism'?

Generally speaking, the 'neo's are open to criticism. But we have to understand how that has come about. Neo-Thomism derived essentially from Leo XIII. He began his pontificate in 1878, on the death of Pius IX, and ended it in 1903 at a great age. So his pontificate ended the nineteenth cenutry, which is a century of Catholic restoration. The Church had been traumatized and deeply wounded by the French revolution, Napoleon and the Napoleonic wars, the dismantling of the principalities and kingdoms of Europe on Napoleon's initiative and the weakness of Catholic intellectualism, apart from names like Lamennais, whose development was very different – sadly, when he had so many and such really prophetic things in him.

Leo XIII was well aware that the Church's institutional restoration would not be complete if there were not a restoration of Catholic intellectualism. That is why, when he had barely been enthroned, he published the famous encyclical in which he called for the expansion of Christian philosophy. First of all he cited St Thomas, but also St Anselm and St Bonaventure, though giving pride of place to St Thomas. From that moment on a school was formed which even in the Dominican province of Paris had teachers from abroad, because we did not have enough on our own staff; thus Zigliara taught some people. Then there was Fr Ambroise Gardeil and Le Saulchoir, founded in Belgium in 1905, which went beyond this somewhat cramped and essentialist Neo-Thomism, if one can describe it in that way, towards history and also towards openness. However, at that point we were in Belgium, quite isolated and very much in the country, and therefore, unfortunately, hardly involved in the exchange of ideas. We all dreamed of returning to France and being relocated near living cultural centres. That happened, but just as war broke out, in 1940.

I think that in many ways Le Saulchoir went beyond this somewhat over-systematic Neo-Thomism. At all events, we never went into Billot's Neo-Thomism with its famous twenty-four theses, all moreover pure philosophy and not theology, whereas Gilson has shown clearly that St Thomas is first and foremost a theologian, even if he did a lot of philosophy. (St

Thomas always gave a course of commentary on Aristotle, but this was restricted to Dominican students.)

Theology can sometimes lead to disagreements with certain magisterial authorities. You yourself have had experience of it. Can there be, for good reasons, a right to disagreement in the Church? Does the new Canon Law leave a place for it?

I cannot say whether the present Canon Law leaves a place for disagreement, but I can say that the theme of *dignitatis humanae personae* on religious liberty is taken up in it, since I've checked that. Otherwise I haven't spent enough time on the new Canon Law to settle that point completely.

I discussed this question of the right to disagreement in a lecture which I gave at the Catholic Institute, which moreover was organized by the Faculty of Canon Law, and my contribution was published in the *Année canonique*. I began with some examples. I can remember two of them. The first was that of Robert Grosseteste, who wrote an extraordinary letter in which he absolutely refused to yield to the Pope; he makes the terse statement *obedienter recuso et rebello* (i.e. it is by refusing and rejecting any submission that I show my obedience). The other example is that of the German Centre Party, asked by Leo XIII, who wanted to make peace with Bismarck after the Kulturkampf, to approve the military laws, which were voted for seven years. And the Centre Party refused. That shows that there are cases in which *obedienter* (in obedience) one may refuse something that authority demands (without, however, imposing it, in the two cases that I have just mentioned).

There would be other cases. That of Luther, among others. He asked questions and was told: 'So you are more intelligent than anyone else? Has no one understood this before you?' Luther asked questions several times and reproached himself for having been too patient rather than not patient enough... There is also the case of Loisy, who thought that what he could see was self-evident – and it has to be remembered what the demands of Roman orthodoxy were at the time on biblical matters: present-day official collections no longer give even the texts! There is also the case of the worker priests who were asked to stop working in factories: it was their Christian and apostolic solidarity that was put in question. Those are real questions.

My conclusion is as follows: one has the right to disagree when one has a duty to disagree, in the name of a recognized truth, whether this is historical biblical truth (Loisy), apostolic truth (worker priests), pastoral truth (Grosseteste) or political truth (the Centre Party). One has the right when one has the duty.

I personally have not experienced such dramatic situations as these, but I have been somewhat 'discriminated against'. At the Council, Cardinal Pellegrino, without mentioning me by name, clearly referred to me when he said: 'There are theologians who once had sanctions against them and were even exiled, and who now are experts to whom we listen'; he told me that he had me in mind (he said the same thing to Fr Chenu). I personally was always obedient to the legal measure which affected me and I gave myself a set period for reflection on the soundness of the position of those who were against me or the criticism that they formulated. There is need for a breathing space, for withdrawal and even for patience, but one has to keep one's freedom of judgment. Once again, one has the right to disagree when one has the duty to, and the duty can only be that of the truth.

However, I would add that if it is a matter of obedience – and clearly I have reflected about this – there are two levels. Moreover that is true of all the vows, including those of chastity and poverty, if one may venture to talk about them. There is a kind of legal and social level, and there is a deeper level, the level of the mystery of salvation. The same goes for obedience: there is the legal aspect, and communion in the mystery of the obedience of Jesus to his Father which made him cry out: 'Father, if it is possible, let this cup pass from me' and 'My God, my God, why have you forsaken me?' I think that it is very important to see that. St Thomas himself, in the *Summa*, speaks of vows in two different contexts: in the virtue of religion (of a more external and social kind) and in contemplative life, as a school of the Lord's service (a very Benedictine formula: Thomas had been an oblate at Monte Cassino between the ages of ten and fourteen. And when I went to that abbey I saw young boys who were there amongst the monks, little Neapolitans boys like he was, chubby and brown).

Ecumenism

How would you now describe your involvement in the ecumenical movement?

Ecumenism has been my concern, I would even say my vocation, for a very long time; it is a vocation that I can date quite precisely from 1929, though it has antecedents, kinds of preparation in my childhood and youth of which I have spoken elsewhere. I even ask myself, often, if I have been faithful to this vocation and this grace. For I accept that it was a grace. I must say that today, when it comes to ecumenism, most of the time I keep asking myself questions. And what I shall go on to say in a moment is the expression of these questions. It would be wrong to take them as so many conclusions, affirmations; rather, they are a reflection which I am attempting and in which I think I am coming close to certain suggestions of my old friend Oscar Cullmann, though I would not identify myself completely with his position. We do not have the same vocabulary, the same starting points or the same training. Finally, it is clear that after centuries of controversies, polemic, explanation, we have not convinced one another. We have not convinced the Protestants, or even the Anglicans or the Orthodox, of our position over the primacy of the Pope. The Protestants have not convinced us over *scriptura sola*, nor will they, and so on. Granted, at present we are engaged in dialogue, and this dialogue often takes us a long way; I am a super-champion of dialogue, of which I have been one of the promoters and in which I have been much involved. But in one sense the result of the dialogue has been, if not to 'imprison', at least to confirm each party in its own tradition. In fact each party affirms its identity in the dialogue and maintains it. In this connection I would refer to the categories used by the 1963 Montreal Faith and Order Conference: the distinction which was made between Tradition and the traditions. Tradition, with a capital T, was the transmission of the *traditum*, the content of the gospel, the content of the Word of God or, more precisely, of revelation; whereas traditions were the historical, basically confessional forms in which each individual receives and lives out the Tradition. In fact we only see Tradition in a tradition. We Roman Catholics, we Westerners, above all we Latins (even if Latinity extends to the Anglo-Saxon world of North America), should have no illusions: we live in our tradition. We receive the Tradition only in our Roman Catholic traditions. That makes me ask myself what the differences in the traditions represent, and as I do so, I am struck by the fact that these differences have not arisen from superficial and purely historical matters, for example from the fact that Luther had a particular temperament, that he lived at a particular time, spoke a particular language, and so on. No, they derive from the source itself, since in fact the confessional traditions are the way in which each individual experiences and receives the fundamental Tradition.

So the differences arise from the source. For example, the Orthodox difference which sets over against the utter primacy of Rome a conciliarity, a conciliar synodical régime, derives from the source itself, and the New Testament is in fact the basis for both. The idea of reformation by exclusive reference to the Bible, which I think needs to be criticized, is nevertheless motivated by the view that everything comes from the Word of God. So the difference itself derives from the source, and it is that which poses extremely serious problems, since in the end one cannot get rid of it. The difference has to be recognized.

This is where I join company once again with the comments made by Oscar Cullmann, who would perhaps talk more in terms of charisma; that is not my vocabulary in this question, but it comes extremely close to it. In *Chrétiens désunis* I used the term 'values'. In St Paul the diversity of charismata goes to make up the life of each local church; the application of this notion to churches that history has separated would seem to me to be very much open to discussion. On the other hand, Cullmann does not attach enough importance to the increasing degree of agreement which is progressively pointing in the direction of a church which accepts differences in life-style and expressions of faith.

And then again, I have often reflected on John 17, since it is to this text that I owe my ecumenical vocation: it was when I was preparing for my ordination as priest in 1929 that while studying the Gospel of John I stopped at chapter 17. Since then God knows how many times I have read it and even prayed it. It is the summary of the very prayer of Jesus. In John 17 Jesus prays for all those who keep his own words through the words of the apostles. And that is basically his Church. So I ask myself whether one cannot extend this notion of Church beyond the confessional form of the Church, however profound and holy it may be. It may be, for example, the Roman Catholic Church; or the Orthodox Church, which is also holy and venerable. I am convinced that there is *one* Church, but is it not larger than what we can see? Since then I have finally asked myself whether we should not ask ourselves once again about this text in John 17. For it says: 'That they may be one as we are one', and in Greek the *as* (we are one) is *kathos*, which does not simply denote an imitation but expresses the source of our own unity. Now the Father, the Son and the Spirit are three hypostases which are distinct as such, but have the same substance and are as one in the other. I think that the term *perichoresis* or circumincession is very important in theology: the persons are as the one in the other. So I ask myself to what degree one should not accept a unity which itself encompasses differences, but differences which, by a dialogue which continues to be extremely open, would be as one in the other, i.e. would not close in on themselves. I envisage a primacy which would not close in on itself but would allow a degree of conciliarity. There is certainly something of that in the life of the Catholic Church today, and among the Orthodox there are those who profess a conception of the conciliarity of the Churches which allows for a primacy, includes the primacy; among Protestants, there are believers who accept that scripture comes down through a tradition and is even enriched in a certain way by the understanding of it which has been developed by a multitude of generations and witnesses in the course of the centuries.

Here I would want to protest against a certain ecclesiological defeatism, a certain lack of ambition. So I am very happy to quote a comment by Max Thurian in connection with *Baptism, Eucharist and Ministry*, which is a perfect example of what I say elsewhere: each Church reads this text in accordance with its own tradition and does not ask itself very hard whether it should not go beyond this confessional historical tradition in order to arrive at a common and deeper source. 'Before going into detail, there is one question that we should all ask ourselves: do we really want unity? One sometimes has the impression that... ecumenism began in 1910 or 1926 and that we have had this experience for more than fifty years... The Catholic Church has got on the train during the journey and now we have to take note of this important "passenger". But I sometimes get the impression that we are sitting in this very comfortable train; perhaps we have got to the dining car, and so on... Fine, but are we really travelling towards visible *unity*, or are we still going to be quite happy for a long time to be travelling side by side, acknowledging our friendship, an immense friendship which is born of these contacts, these relationships...?' So Thurian is asking here whether we are really looking for unity. In its various declarations, in particular the Nairobi declaration (which was one of the strongest) and more recently in the Vancouver declaration, the World Council is formally pronouncing that it wants visible unity. And basically, its concept of conciliar unity – perhaps somewhat obsure and debatable, but in the end most eloquent – is almost what we understand by the communion of local churches in an absolute unity of profound faith, sacramentality and ministry. So the World Council constantly proclaims its concern for unity. But is that what we really want? Is that what we are really looking for? I sometimes ask myself.

I am well aware of the progress being made. I am well aware of the work of joint commissions, either at first hand – I was at

80

the very first meeting of all and then I became too ill to continue, but I followed developments all the same – or indirectly through my friends who are members of these commissions, to know that progress with Lutherans has gone a very long way. That is perhaps one of the results of our great progress in understanding Luther, which has really been demonstrated by the publications of the Luther year, 1983. So I think that there will be acts of unity which also recognize the diversity, and you know how fond the Lutherans are of the expression 'reconciled diversities'. Perhaps it is a somewhat debatable expression, but one can give an exact meaning to it, and basically I am very near to accepting its content.

That is what I can say from an ecumenical perspective today. Once again, these are questions that I ask myself, or should I say that my thoughts end up in questioning, rather than in affirmation. I began with a proper Thomistic training, which I would not want to be without because it is good training for the mind; and I began with solid affirmations. It was the idea of Catholicity which at the time seemed to me to encompass the diversities; today I am more aware of the diversities, as is evident from my recent book *Diversity and Communion*.

This book, which is the text of lectures I gave at the Catholic Institute, contains more questions than solutions. But let me outline a conclusion. I recommend a reference to the common basis of our origins. It is not a matter of a freshening up, or attempting an impossible reconstruction of, the Church of the time of the Fathers, but of recognizing together, as a necessary and sufficient condition of communion, the essentials of the faith and order of the Church of the Fathers and the first seven ecumenical councils. That will requires a great confessional conversion from all of us. Is that a mirage? But who is putting forward any other synthesis? And what is it?

I will be asked what role the papacy would have in this perspective. Earlier, I expressed my conviction, which has a solid basis, that the Church of Jesus Christ and the apostles includes a ministry of Peter: a mission and a charge, with charismas and corresponding powers. Today many Protestants accept the idea of a personalized ministry of universal unity. So do Anglicans. Cardinal Ratzinger has written on several occasions that we must not impose on the Orthodox more than the affirmations and the *modus vivendi* of the period before 1054. And our papacy can follow the model of Gregory the Great and John XXIII... So is the prospect really hopeless?

But there is work to be done and grace to be prayed for!

Since our focus is now on questions of theology, how do you regard what has emerged over recent years with the 'theologies of liberation'?

I am acquainted with a certain number of well-known authors of this theology of liberation. I have close personal connections with Gustavo Gutiérrez, and I know Leonardo Boff extremely well. I know others like Pablo Richard, but there are also those whom I do not know personally, like Sobrino. You will realize that their intention is to replace the theology of development on which Paul VI based his fine encyclical *Populorum progressio*, which owes a good deal to Fr Lebret. The basic idea and whole phrases come from Fr Lebret. But there is more here than development, because the very idea of liberation has come from the awareness of a whole people which is both poor and Christian, that they must liberate themselves. That has been the starting point of this theology. What I have against some ideas, some accounts, and even the very first accounts by Ratzinger (I'm not referring to the last text, of Easter 1976 or 1978), is that they connect liberation theology with European origins. Now it is true that Leonardo Boff studied in Germany, and indeed with Ratzinger, whose pupil he was, and that Gustavo Gutiérrez studied in Lyons. But that does not make liberation theology an application of European political theology, and if the liberation theologians have taken over certain concepts, even from Marxism – and have done so, moreover, in a way which can be and has been rightly criticized – that is not the real origin of their researches. The true source of liberation theology is the specific experience of a poor Christian people which is aware of its situation and of its concern to free itself – on the basis of the gospel itself and in small basic communities. This is so basic that it produces a kind of epistemological structure which is not that of theological reflection of a Western kind, but is original. It is that which in my view has not been sufficiently recognized, even in Rome.

And now I come to the Roman document on the question. The first document was very much criticized and somewhat negative. But it is above all the second document that I want to talk about, since it takes things much further. This is the document of 22 March 1986 on *Freedom and Liberation*. This seems to me to be a very interesting development. In some respects I would compare it to that of John-Paul II in his encyclical on work (*Laborem exercens*) in which the Pope goes from work, work in itself, to the worker. Similarly, here it is significant that the document goes from liberation in itself, as a political result, as socio-political action, to human beings. Clearly there is a danger of moralizing liberation, somehow forgetting the social and political demands which are nevertheless quite essential, and putting the main stress on individual moral demands: freedom in its depths, freedom from sin, as if everything stemmed from sin. Now of course in a sense everything has its roots in human pride, ambition and a desire for power. But in the end everything does not stem from there. There are nevertheless external conditions which must rightly be taken into account. And the liberation theologians have taken them into account, often using concepts which they have not criticized enough. In particular there is one that I consider very dangerous and that needs to be rejected: the Marxist concept of class struggle, since its effect is really to stir up class struggle systematically. We have to recognize that beyond question there is a tension, even conflict, here, indeed that there are class conflicts. But that is something that has not been criticized.

I recall the hour and three quarters that I once spent with Lopez Trujillo, who has since become a cardinal. He is an enemy of liberation theology and he quoted extracts from books by Gutiérrez in particular, Marxist-type passages which were quotations from Marx or had a Marxist stamp. Certainly there was good reason to criticize them or to ask for them to be made more precise, to criticize even their conceptuality, and I believe that liberation theologians are doing precisely that. There is amazing good will among them. With a person like Leonardo Boff there is even a Franciscan spirit, a somewhat anarchical spiritual freedom, if you like, which has led him to take positions on other theological questions which I have criticized at one time or another from an ecclesiological or Mariological point of view. I regret these positions in a theologian who, moreover, has had a good training and has real class.

Finally, I would add that liberation theology cannot be transposed elsewhere as it is. I am well aware that at present it is being transposed to some degree to Africa, but there it will be very different. It cannot be transposed to Europe because the situation is quite different. We are not dealing with a poor Christian people which is basically religious; we are dealing with intellectuals, with political movements structured into real parties, and that is quite different. On the other hand, I believe that this liberation theology has a message for all the Churches, and I am glad that it has often been allowed to find expression in the journal *Concilium* (whole numbers, then a whole section), because one would think that the Churches which numerically speaking will soon represent a third of world Catholicism have something to say to others, and that these Christian experiences expressed by liberation theologians have a message for us. In this respect I think that they have a general value, even if they cannot be transposed everywhere.

In these years leading up to the third millennium, how do you see the future of Christianity?

First of all I should point out that the question is about Christianity, so that it goes beyond the Roman Catholic Church. We must envisage not only the chances of vitality for other Churches, but the opportunities which would occur for Christianity through the fact of a union of Churches 'that the world may believe'.

As far as Catholicism is concerned, I recently collected a certain number of statements dating from the first third of the nineteenth century announcing that it would soon disappear. Such forecasts were made in a period which had a lively awareness of its modernity and in comparison with which Catholicism seemed hopelessly outmoded. Now two apparently contrary but in fact parallel movements are in play in Catholicism: on the one hand adaptation, a more or less difficult and chaotic welcome to modernity (at least in part); and on the other hand the reinforcement and affirmation of Christian (Catholic) identity. Nowadays that is taking the form of the dynamism of John-Paul II, the extension of the need for spirituality and prayer groups ('renewal'), the vitality of scholarship and publications on academic theology. There are enough results to make probable (reasonable) a positive if not optimistic response to the question of the future of Catholicism, at least in terms of the facts. After that comes the reply of faith and theological hope, but also Jesus' question: 'When the Son of Man returns, will he still find faith on the earth?'

By way of a conclusion

I hope that the reader will not see these open conversations as anything other than or more than they were. This is not an elaborate work, nor are its statements in any way definitive. These are improvised responses to questions put in friendship, at the beginning of the evening, to someone who has been in hospital since 9 October 1984. I try to keep up to date, but I can only do so in a partial and disjointed way. I do not have that exchange of ideas which would allows me to complete or correct anything in my suggestions which is probably open to question. I can certainly say now, two years after the beginning of these conversations, that sometimes I could have expressed myself better, since one learns all the time. And since then, there have been many publications, the Holy Father's visit to France and the meeting between the religions in Assisi on 27 October 1986.

Nowadays I can hardly write anything. However, as in what I have written and published, I have put something of my soul into this book.

Withdrawn from active life, I am united to the mystical body of the Lord Jesus of which I have often spoken. I am united to it, day and night, by the prayer of one who has also known his share of suffering.

I have a keen awareness of the vast dimensions of the mystical body. By and in the Holy Spirit I am present to its members, known (to me) and unknown. Ecumenism obviously plays a part in this. It is intercession, consolation, thanksgiving, as the Lord wills.